CREATIVE BIBLE LESSONS IN Galatians & Philippians

12 sessions on grace, growth, freedom, and faith

CREATIVE BIBLE LESSONS IN Galatians & Philippians

12 sessions on grace, growth, freedom, and faith

TIM McLAUGHLIN & J. CHERI McLAUGHLIN
JIM MILLER & YOLANDA MILLER

A DIVISION OF HARPERCOLLINS*PUBLISHERS*

Creative Bible Lesson in Galatians and Philippians: 12 sessions on grace, growth, freedom, and faith

Youth Specialties Books, 300 S. Pierce St., El Cajon, CA 92020, are published by Zondervan Publishing House, 5300 Patterson Ave. S.E., Grand Rapids, MI 49530.

Library of Congress Cataloging-in-Publication Data

Miller, Jim, 1971-
Creative Bible lessons in Galatians and Philippians : 12 studies on freedom, passions, grace, and joy / Jim Miller & Yolanda Miller.
p. cm.
ISBN 0-310-23177-9 (alk. paper)
1. Bible. N.T. Galatians—Study and teaching (Secondary) 2. Bible. N.T. Philippians—Study and teaching (Secondary) 3. Christian education of teenagers. I. Miller, Yolanda, 1972- II. Title.

BS2685.55 .M55 2001
227′.4′00712—dc21

2001017722

Written by Tim McLaughlin and J. Cheri McLaughlin with contributions by Jim Miller and Yolanda Miller
Edited by Lorna McFarland Hartman
Cover and interior design by Jack Rogers

Printed in the United States of America

01 02 03 04 05 06 07 / / 10 9 8 7 6 5 4 3 2 1

St. Paul's Letter to the Galatians

St. Paul's Letter to the Philippians

welcome to

Creative Bible Lessons in Galatians & Philippians!

You're a youth worker—which is to say, you'd rather be hanging with students or teaching them than reading introductions to a curriculum.

So let's cut to the chase. The idea behind this curriculum is simple: *Lead adolescents into understanding a couple of St. Paul's letters, allowing the letters to speak for themselves instead of imposing an artificial theme on them.*

That's the short form. Here's another-but-still-short form:

If you're looking for an introduction to Paul's letters, Galatians and Philippians make a good pair of letters to start with. Here's why:

- They're both on the brief side (six and four chapters, respectively). After all, students stampede for *The Old Man and the Sea* if the only alternative is *Moby Dick*, right? Besides, the study of a couple of short letters fits conveniently into a typical youth ministry programming calendar.

- Galatians and Philippians convey entirely different tones. Paul patterned his letter to the Galatians after legal treatises of his day. Philippians, on the other hand, is an intimate letter that follows the heart's tangents rather than some strict organization—which drives theologians crazy.

- Despite their different tones, they overlap on one conspicuous topic: whether being circumcised in order to be a true Christian is necessary. Probably not a big controversy in your youth group, but it was *huge* in the first decades of the church. And if you step back and take a larger view, you'll see that the issue is not circumcision, but one of the plagues Christianity has suffered since its beginning: the "Christianity and..." syndrome. Sure, we may *say* that God's grace is all one needs in order to become part of his family and receive eternal life, but sooner or later, many groups introduce another requirement, if not for salvation, then for good standing in their churches: baptism of whatever kind or a "biblical" view (read, the church's view) of a sociopolitical issue—abortion, school prayer, political affiliation, biblical interpretation. In the first century, what completed the "Christianity and..." was circumcision for all believers in Jesus, whether Jew or non-Jew, probably because that male-only rite was the primary and visible sign that one was part of God's chosen people, the Jews.

- The Jew Paul tore into that reasoning like lions into Christians when he said, "You just don't get it, do you?" He wrote that the only kind of circumcision that *ever* counted was the circumcision of the heart—that is, a *heart* marked for God. The same argument needs to be heard today. Do we really believe that, fundamentally, our Christianness is a matter of the heart, and not necessarily of a measurable, visible sign?

So you get a feeling for how confrontational these letters can be. Anyway, that's why Galatians and Philippians are heaped together, though studied separately, in this curriculum.

Each session's components and how to use them

- Sessions begin with an enlightening **essay** for you about the featured Bible passage. It familiarizes the biblically unlearned with the issue at hand, gives seasoned Bible teachers what is probably a fresh perspective of the passage, and in any case contains interesting stuff that you can use in teaching your high schoolers the session to come.

- Then choose from a couple of **Openers**—usually a festive one and a calmer one.

- **In the Book** follows the same pattern. You can conduct the main Bible study portion of the session one of two ways—the **small group Bible-snooping option** is the standard, plus there's an option that gets kids into the passage in a more unusual way.

- The **Closing** is—well, the closing. Often a group prayer, but hardly always. In one session we recommend a Steve Taylor song as a benediction.

Session 1

More Than You Thought You Needed to Know about Jewish Customs

Galatians (yes, the whole book)
Genesis 15-17
Exodus 23:20-24:18

During this session students will—

- Recognize that the root of Christianity is Judaism, as unfolded in the Hebrew Bible (the Christian's Old Testament).
- Feel the tension of early Christ-followers as they sorted out which acts and teachings from their religious heritage were fulfilled in Jesus Christ, therefore freeing them from carrying the burden of flawless obedience to the whole Law of Moses.

Get in the Galatians mood

Read the entire book of Galatians at one sitting in *The Message* (Eugene H. Petersen, NavPress), the Contemporary English Version of the New Testament (American Bible Society), or another contemporary language translation of the Bible.

Here are a few zinger quotes from the apostle Paul in *The Message* to shake you into the read-through—

- "As for those who were considered important in the church, their reputation doesn't concern me. God isn't impressed with mere appearances, and neither am I. And of course these leaders were able to add nothing to the message I had been preaching."
- "This great Message I delivered to you is not mere human optimism. I didn't receive it through the traditions, and I wasn't taught it in some school. I got it straight from God, received the Message directly from Jesus Christ."
- "I am emphatic about this. The moment any one of you submits to circumcision or any other rule-keeping system, at that same moment Christ's hard-won gift of freedom is squandered."
- "When you attempt to live by your own religious plans and projects, you are cut off from Christ, you fall out of grace."
- "Why don't these agitators, obsessive as they are about circumcision, go all the way and castrate themselves!"
- "Why don't you choose to be led by the spirit and so escape the erratic compulsions of a law-dominated existence?"
- "I am set free from the stifling atmosphere of pleasing others and fitting into the little patterns that they dictate."

Inform your teaching
About this letter...

Paul's letter to the Galatians, among the most important of early Christian writings, affirms salvation by grace alone—a salvation apart from the Law of Moses, so that believers are free to serve one another in love.

This letter is more than a Magna Carta of spiritual emancipation, more than what Martin Luther called "his epistle" (in Luther's commentary on Galatians, he described himself as married to the letter). This letter can reveal Paul as a soulmate to your students: his teachings in Galatians on the law and grace, on spiritual childhood and adulthood, on how one can navigate this terrain—this is precisely what adolescents are dealing with as they struggle to differentiate and individuate themselves from their parents and other "laws" that govern their childhood.

In short, Paul's letter to the Galatian Christians is a passionate defense of his gospel, which says that we live for God only by faith in Jesus Christ and not by performing the Jewish law—or any other law that says we earn our place in God's salvation by what we do.

What we know, what we don't know

Scholars aren't certain—

- How the chronologies of Galatians sync with the Acts stories of Paul's journeys.
- Whether Paul wrote to the churches in northern or southern Galatia.
- Whether he wrote it in A.D. 49 before the ruling of the council at Jerusalem regarding Christian freedom from the Law of Moses or in A.D. 56 after the council had spoken.

What we *do* know with fair certainty—

- Paul made several trips into Asia Minor, where Turkey is today, and helped set up churches throughout the region—including churches in northern and southern Galatia, a Roman-owned territory since 25 B.C.
- New Christians in those churches were being persuaded that believers had to be circumcised before they were *really* right with God.
- Paul had heard that those to whom he had preached were questioning whether he had taught them the true gospel.
- Paul, passionately distraught for his converts' spiritual safety and irate at the false teachers (called Judaizers), writes his letter to the churches in Galatia to sort out the mess.

Opener [simulation option]

It's tough to break a two-millennium habit

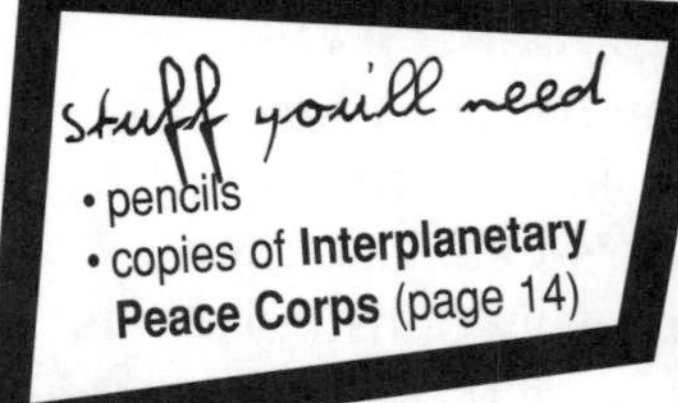
stuff you'll need
• pencils
• copies of Interplanetary Peace Corps (page 14)

As students settle down, start handing out **Interplanetary Peace Corps** (page 14) and say—

Exploring the Bible can feel alien to those of us who aren't scholars. What would it feel like if you were attempting to communicate Earth ideas and customs to people on another planet?

Form groups of no more than five to run through this 10-minute simulation of just such an experience. One member can record the group's ideas on her handout, and one member can summarize the exercise when the group gathers together again.

Brief the group on the simulation. Then

transition to a second opener or to an **In the Book** option by saying—

God had the task of forming a people who would bring his message of salvation to the world. It certainly hasn't gone off without a hitch.

Opener [game option]

Dicing the dictionary

stuff you'll need
- pencils
- copies of **Dicing the Dictionary** (page 15) for each student

Once students settle, distribute **Dicing the Dictionary** (page 15). Let your students know whether you want them to complete the sheet independently or in groups. Say something like—

We're beginning a study of Paul's letter to the Galatians. That means we're in for an adventure with words and concepts rooted in Paul's Jewish upbringing. Just for fun, let's start with a little word play ourselves. Using the handout and conferring with someone sitting near you, discuss for five minutes the meaning of some distinctive words.

Here are the answers (as if you really need them).

- **circumcision**—the removal of foreskin
- **Jews**—all of the above (people who worshiped God, who was known then as *Yahweh*...people who were God's chosen...people who used to be known as Hebrews or Israelites)
- **Gentiles**—people who were not Jews
- **justification**—being pronounced legally innocent of wrongdoing
- **righteousness**—following divine or moral law
- **emasculate**—castrate
- **revelation**—all of the above (a book of the Bible...a giving of knowledge...a sudden awareness)
- **redeem**—free someone by paying their ransom
- **covenant**—a binding agreement
- **transgression**—a sin
- **mediator**—a person who acts as a bridge between others
- **gospel**—all of the above (good news...the story of Jesus Christ...a type of music)

In the Book [impromptu panel option]

S.W.W.F. (Spiritual World Wrestling Federation)

stuff you'll need
- four copies of **S.W.W.F. (Spiritual World Wrestling Federation)** (page 16)

For this pre-fight interview with Abraham Road Dog, Moses the Slasher, and Big Boss Man Paul, you'll need the help of three students. The readers have to be able to put out the raw-meat hype of World Wrestling Federation stars and announcers. It works best with a quick rehearsal—though if your student actors are naturals, they can probably do it impromptu.

When you've completed the reading, you could say something like—

The tension between WWF competitors is, of course, staged. The tension between Paul and Jewish Christians who were polluting the message of salvation by grace through faith alone was real and complex. As we read most of Galatians in the next few weeks, you'll hear Paul rabidly defend his gospel message and his authority to preach the gospel. He'll even stoop to name-calling and calling curses down on the agitators. It could seem very much like the interview we just heard—in

fact, most of the words of Abraham, Moses, and Paul were right out of *The Message*, an in-your-face translation of the Bible.

In the Book
[small group Bible-snooping option]

What's this "gospel" Paul is so fired up about?

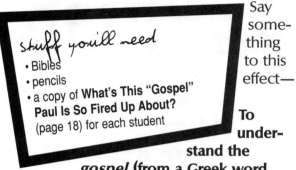

stuff you'll need
- Bibles
- pencils
- a copy of **What's This "Gospel" Paul Is So Fired Up About?** (page 18) for each student

Say something to this effect—

To understand the *gospel* (from a Greek word that means *good news*) you first need to understand what *covenants* are—especially what covenants meant to first-century Jews.

To make a covenant with someone means to be in agreement with that person about pledges made to each other. Covenants, or alliances of friendship, between individuals or nations have always been accompanied by solemn rituals—choosing a sign or symbol of the covenant, making a sacrifice, and taking an oath to keep the covenant.

Those who enter into a covenant together expect benefits to come to them. Those who break covenants expect punishment—even death. In ancient times covenant rituals included killing an animal, which as much as said, "If I don't do what I've said I'll do, make me like this animal."

Everything God does is based on covenant. If you think back over Bible stories you know, you'll find lots of covenant making.

- **God made a covenant with the whole earth in front of Noah after the flood, promising to never destroy the earth again by a flood. His solemn sign was the rainbow.**

- **Abraham and God entered into a covenant that was one-sided—from God to Abraham—assuring Abraham of descendants numbering more than the stars. The solemn sign was several animals cut in half that God passed between while Abraham slept.**

- **Moses mediated a covenant between God and Israel when he received the stone tablets on Mt. Sinai. The solemn sign was animal blood sprinkled over all the people and the book of the covenant.**

- **Prince Jonathan made a covenant with David to defend him from his enemies. His solemn sign was buckling his sword on David's waist.**

- **God later made a covenant with the same David that there would always be a king from his family ruling over Israel. His solemn symbol was that God's love would never leave David or David's descendants—of whom Jesus is one.**

- **Jesus started what he called the New Covenant at dinner with his disciples the night before he died. His solemn symbol was the bread he passed around and the cup of wine they shared together.**

The idea of a covenant with God is a Jewish tradition that has become central to Christianity too.

In small groups, let's talk more about

how parts of Israel's history inform our Christian faith.

Form small groups of five to 10 people and give them pencils, Bibles, and **What's This "Gospel" Paul Is So Fired Up About?** (page 18). Make sure they or you read the simple instructions at the top of the sheet.

Closing

Jewish prayer, the origin of Christian liturgy

Your church may regularly recite a version of the Lord's prayer during worship services. If so, your students may already know it. For groups unfamiliar with the prayer, print it on poster board or an overhead so everyone participating feels certain they'll say the correct words. Say to the students—

Among the gifts to Christianity from Hebrew worship of the living God is the format for the Lord's Prayer. From the "Our Father," which mirrors the Jewish understanding of God as our Father, to the closing worship in the phrase "Thine is the power and glory forever, amen," this prayer that Jesus taught his disciples fit in with the way they were used to praying as devout Jews. We'll pause till next week in our study of Galatians by saying the Lord's Prayer together.

Interplanetary Peace Corps

It's the far distant future when young adults routinely serve on interplanetary service missions.

In two months your team will be leaving for an extended stay on a planet among a people whose population has been decimated by tribal warfare and a superstition-based religion. They are scientifically illiterate, so they regularly sacrifice their strongest and most beautiful to appease the gods of sun, rain, harvest, and fertility. They have no idea of planets, let alone that beings like themselves could travel through space to help them.

Your goal is to bring peace among the tribes and educate them to live in their world wisely and safely. Your first task will be to form a coalition of members from at least one tribe, and to introduce an appropriate ritual that will cement their loyalty to the coalition, and be a symbol identifying them to all others. As individuals from any tribe join the coalition—and your goal is for *all* the peoples to join together—they will participate in the same ritual.

- Describe the ritual your team chooses.

- What about this ritual will cement loyalty, as opposed to merely interesting people in what you're doing?

- How will your team participate in this ritual?

Dicing the dictionary

Circle or check the definition that makes most sense to you. Or cross out the definitions that make least sense to you. Or write, cast, and stage a musical comedy that uses eight of these 12 terms. Or, of course, you can just talk about them.

circumcision
- ☐ a circular cut
- ☐ a circular saw
- ☐ the removal of foreskin
- ☐ a knight named Komcision

Jews
- ☐ people who worshiped God, who was also known as "Yahweh"
- ☐ people who were God's chosen
- ☐ people who also used to be known as Hebrews or Israelites
- ☐ all of the above

Gentiles
- ☐ people who were not Jews
- ☐ people who were gentle
- ☐ people who were sissies
- ☐ all of the above

justification
- ☐ to be declared legally innocent of wrongdoing
- ☐ the act of taking a vacation
- ☐ the act of making a rude noise
- ☐ the act of making up an excuse

righteousness
- ☐ the habit of turning to the right
- ☐ the habit of repeatedly saying, "RIGHTEOUS!"
- ☐ being right-handed
- ☐ following divine or moral law

emasculate
- ☐ make into a man
- ☐ castrate
- ☐ wear a mask and be late
- ☐ have body odor

revelation
- ☐ a book of the Bible
- ☐ a giving of knowledge
- ☐ a sudden awareness
- ☐ all of the above

redeem
- ☐ stick a coupon on someone's forehead
- ☐ free someone by paying their ransom
- ☐ deem someone again
- ☐ spank someone really hard

covenant
- ☐ an ark
- ☐ a type of cove
- ☐ a binding agreement
- ☐ a witches' gathering

transgression
- ☐ a sin
- ☐ a train to Gression
- ☐ a change of clothes
- ☐ a form of oatmeal

mediator
- ☐ a person who is related to a gladiator
- ☐ a person who has ear wax
- ☐ a person who works in the media
- ☐ a person who acts as a bridge between others

gospel
- ☐ good news
- ☐ the story of Jesus Christ
- ☐ a type of music
- ☐ all of the above

Prefight interview with—
- Abraham Road Dog
- Moses the Slasher
- Big Boss Man Paul

Moderated by—
- Youth leader

To be read with the fervency usually reserved for the World Wrestling Federation stars and announcers.

Youth leader: Good evening, ladies and gentlemen. We have with us tonight three of the top celebrities in the Spiritual World Wrestling Federation. The man all Jews and Palestinians call father, the spiritual father of all Christ-followers, and the friend of God—Abraham Road Dog, the faithful.

Abraham: All I know is God said to me, "I am God almighty! I will greatly increase your numbers. You and your family rule! My agreement to back you is forever. And I give you the name Abraham Road Dog because you'll be on the circuit for me, heading for the Promised Land." Yeah!

[Genesis 17:1-8]

Youth leader: Thank you, Father Abraham—uh, Road Dog.

Across the room is revered religious leader of Middle Eastern peoples, divine law giver, writer of the first five books of the Bible, and the only person who's talked with God face to face and lived—Moses the Slasher.

[Exodus 3:11]

Moses: This same God of Abraham told me, "I'm guarding your way until you get to the Promised Land. I will be an enemy to any who oppose you and wipe them out! I will send terror ahead of you and throw your enemies into confusion." Now that's what I'm talking 'bout!

[Exodus 23:20-27]

Youth leader: And finally, the referee for the upcoming matches between Road Dog and the Slasher, the man who articulated the relationship of Abraham's faith with Moses' Law for Christ-followers—Big Boss Man Paul, the apostle.

Paul: The rumor that I continue to preach the ways of the Slasher—circumcision—is absurd. Why, then, would I still be booed out of the ring by fans of the Slasher? If I were preaching that old message, no one would be offended if I mentioned Road Dog's faith in some watered-down, staged TV coverage. Why don't these slavish groupies of the Slasher—obsessive as they are about circumcision—go all the way and castrate themselves! [Galatians 5, *The Message*]

Youth leader: Wait a minute. How can you be a fair referee in the fight between Road Dog and the Slasher when you're so obviously a Road Dog fan?

Paul: Because the Slasher's fans have completely missed the point God made with the Slasher by requiring Christ's followers to be circumcised. The motives of these heretical fans is rotten. They want SWWF fighters everywhere to always depend on them for managing the Spiritual World Wrestling fights so that they'll feel important. And they want every contestant to be cut, according to their rules, to qualify before God as a Spiritual World Wrestler, when God's qualifications are simply to come to him through faith alone. [Galatians 4, *The Message*]

Youth leader: There's no question about it. These next few weeks of competition between Road Dog and his path of faith, and the Slasher's apparent requirement for circumcision, are going to be passionately emceed for us by the Boss Man. Thank you, gentlemen.

Abraham: I'm not afraid to say it right out loud. I was slashed—er, circumcised. But that whole bit came after I believed God. It was when I believed God that he told me he counted me as righteous. [Genesis 15:6; 17:9-13]

Paul: That's right. Keeping rules—even when they're rules God himself makes—doesn't mean you're livin' by faith. [Galatians 3]

Youth leader: Thank you, Big Boss Man.

Paul: Because of Christ's sacrifice, Road Dog's blessing of being in the family that rules is available for all wrestlers and fans. [Galatians 3]

Youth leader: Yes, well it's time to—

Paul: I'm talking here, okay? I'm sayin' we're all able to receive God's life, his Spirit, in and with us, by believing—just the way Road Dog received it. [Galatians 3]

Youth leader: Uh, that's it for this week, fans—unless, uh, any of our guests have anything else to say...

Paul, Moses, Abraham: *(ad lib)* Us? No, nothin' more I wanna say...Nope, that's it for me...Can't think of anything at the moment...How 'bout you, huh?

What's this "gospel" Paul is so fired up about?

Check out how America's most popular holidays got their start (Hallmark should be grateful).

The **Easter bunny** was introduced to American folklore by German settlers who arrived in the Pennsylvania Dutch country during the 18th century. The children believed that if they were good, the "Oschter Haws" would lay a nest of colored eggs.

The American **Santa Claus** grew out of the tradition of a Dutch legend of Sinter Klaas, brought by settlers to New York in the 17th century.

Halloween history includes the ancient Celtic people dressing up in costumes on October 31 to confuse and ward off evil spirits.

What traditions that you honor had their start in some other culture or way of life?

Genesis 15:1-6 and Genesis 17:1-14
OR
Exodus 19:3-8 and Exodus 24:3-8

Choose the Genesis covenant or the Exodus covenant, then talk about some of these questions regarding the covenant you chose. You may want to jot down some insights your group comes up with, or something memorable that one of you says.

- Who was involved in the covenant?

- What seemed to prompt the covenant?

- How long would the covenant last?

- What promises were made?

- Did this covenant have a solemn sign? If so, what was it?

If you chose the Exodus covenant, now read Matthew 26:26-28 and talk about this question:

- What seeds from God's covenant with Israel show up full-grown in Jesus' new covenant?

Enter Paul on the gospel stage
Now that you see how the stage is set for the gospel of salvation by grace through faith in Jesus Christ, read Acts 13:16-39.

- Verse 26: To whom is Paul giving his message of salvation?

- Verses 27-30: To what is Paul referring when he says "they carried out all that was written about Jesus"?

- Paul clearly saw Jesus' coming as the fulfillment of God's promises of salvation to Israel and all humankind. What steps in Israel's history led up to Jesus coming as the savior?

Now read Colossians 2:9-15.

- How does the message that Paul is preaching in Acts 13:38-39 fit in with what he wrote in Colossians 2:13-14 about Christians being circumcised by Christ as a result of his death and resurrection?

Finally...

- Anything in these verses that's a puzzle to you? That just doesn't make sense?

- What one thing got your attention most of all in these verses? Why did it affect you the way it did?

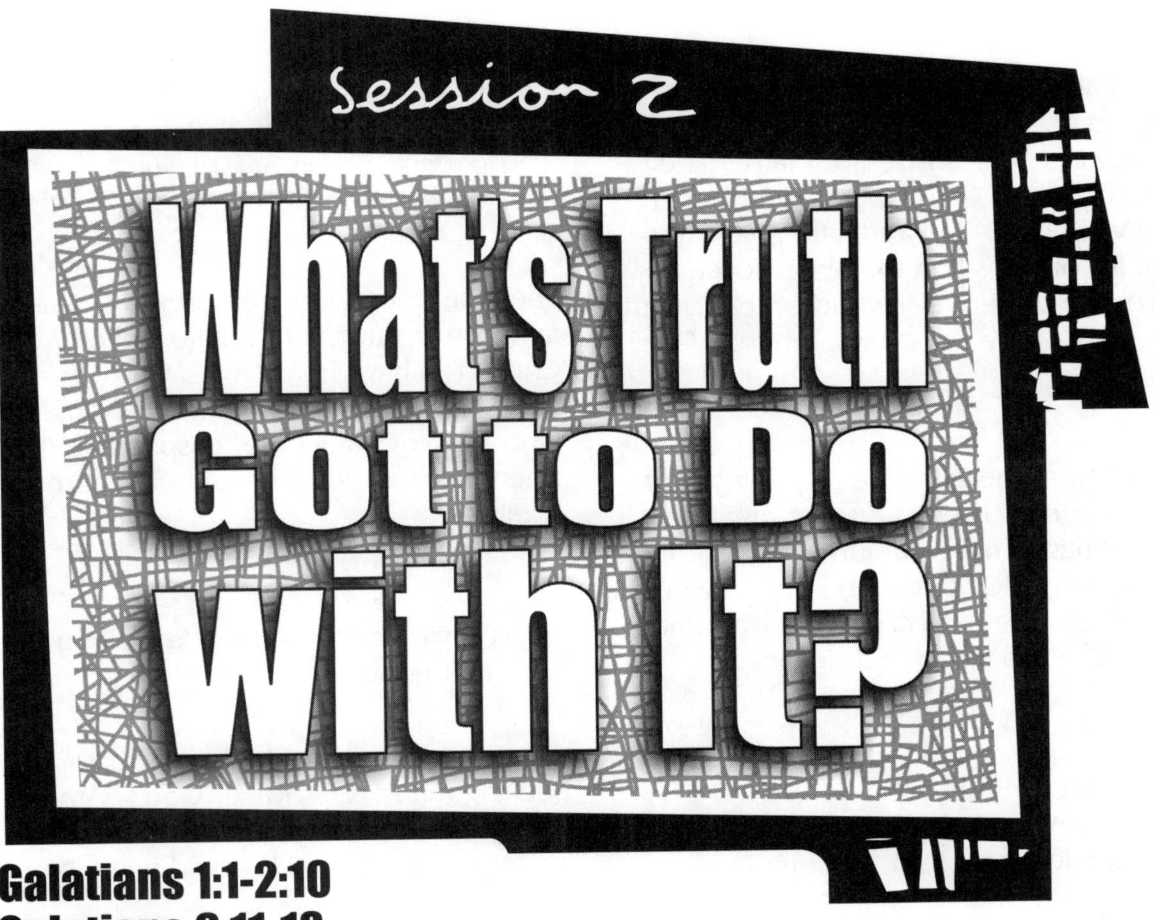

Session 2
What's Truth Got to Do with It?

Galatians 1:1-2:10
Galatians 6:11-18

During this session students will—

- Relate Paul's defense of his credentials as an apostle of Jesus Christ to a defense of the authority of the gospel of freedom he preached.
- Feel Paul's passion for the gospel of salvation by faith alone through reading his personal defense.

Take a walk in Paul's shoes

Thoughtfully read Galatians 1:1 to 2:10 and 6:11-18. You can't understand Galatians apart from Paul's conversion story. That's why he spent almost a third of the letter retelling it.

Next, compare what you read in Galatians with his story as recorded in Acts 9:1-31 and 22:2-23:11.

Finally, read Paul's statement of the gospel in Acts 13:32-39.

Now can you put the gospel according to Paul into one sentence?

Inform your teaching
An e-mail message from Paul

To: Galatians
From: Paul
Subject: Now I'm steamed

>Hiya Paul.

I am Paul, appointed and commissioned a messenger not by man but by Jesus Christ and God the father (who raised him from the dead).

[Galatians 1:1]

>Virtual greetings from the Galatian
>churches—you know, Iconium,
>Lystra, Derbe, and the rest.

[Acts 14:1, 8, 20]

I and all the brothers with me send greetings to the churches in Galatia. Grace and peace to you from God our father and the Lord Jesus Christ, who according to the will of our God and father gave himself for our sins and thereby rescued us from the present evil world-order. To him be glory for ever and ever. Amen.

[Galatians 1:2-5]

>Remember how fired up things got
>when you showed up at the
>synagogue in Iconium, and when
>you healed that man in Lystra whose
>feet were too crippled to walk and
>talked to the crowds in Derbe?

[Acts 14:1-7 (Iconium),
Acts 14:8-10 (Lystra)]

>
>Both Jews and Gentiles started
>believing your gospel—that we have
>forgiveness of sins through Jesus,
>whom God raised from the dead,
>and that through him we can be
>justified from everything we could
>not be justified from by the Law of
>Moses.

[Acts 13:32-39 (Paul's gospel)]

>
>It was so cool how everyone got so
>excited—that is, I mean, the *good*
>excitement. Bummer about the
>Iconium Jews stoning you and all.
>But hey—you warned us on your
>way back home that we'd go
>through a lot of hardships to enter
>the kingdom of God.

[Acts 14:19-20;
Acts 14:22 (hardships)]

>
>By the way. Those same Jews who
>were jealous about the crowds you
>drew keep causing trouble. When
>they saw that bad-mouthing your
>gospel wasn't breaking up the
>meetings of us Christ-followers, they
>shifted tactics. Now they're saying,
>"What Paul was preaching is all right
>to a point. But if you quit following
>the law and refuse to be circumcised,
>all that Jesus stuff won't leave you a
>leg to stand on before God."

[Acts 13:44-45]

There are men who are upsetting your faith with a travesty of the gospel of Christ. You have heard me say it before and now I say it again—may anybody who preaches any other gospel than the one you have already heard be a damned soul!

[Galatians 1:7-9]

>They're saying you made it all up to
>look good.

Does that make you think now that I am seeking man's approval or God's? Am I trying to please men? If I were trying to win human approval I should never be Christ's servant.

[Galatians 1:10]

>They're claiming the authority of the
>temple priests and the authority of
>the law itself.

I do assure you, my brothers, that the gospel I preached to you is no human invention. No man gave it to me, no man taught it to me; it came to me as a direct revelation from Jesus Christ.

[Galatians 1:11-13, Acts 9:1-31, and
22:2-23:11, the long version
of Paul's testimony]

>And people are believing it!

I am amazed that you have so quickly transferred your allegiance from him who called you by the grace of Christ to another "gospel"!

[Galatians 1:6]

Opener [game option]

Truth or lie?

stuff you'll need
- Nothing besides three students, preferably volunteers

Have some group fun with this "parlor game"—it's like the old "Truth or Consequences" TV game show—that should illustrate the difficulty of discerning the truth among various claimants.

Three students leave the room together. Volunteers are best, though you may

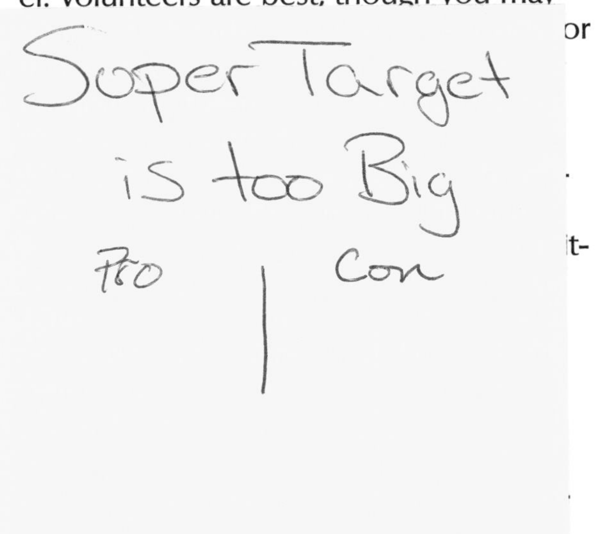

Opener [debate option]

Pro and con

stuff you'll need
- A lectern or music stand

Give your group a chance to interact about a current topic of conversation that is truly controversial. Avoid topics your church or group feels strongly about as an organization—you won't get much debate on these, unless the student arguing the unpopular side isn't worried about being ostracized or asked in for pastoral counseling. Here are some pro-or-con topics to get your juices flowing:

- Christians should not read or study novels whose characters are witches, wizards, or other beings with magical powers.
- The youth group should shut down in order for its Christian members to infiltrate school clubs, teams, groups, and so on, and let our lights shine there.
- Our town should make the meadow west of the city limits into a WalMart.
- We should increase the number of deacons/elders in our church.
- Cleveland High School should go back to holding varsity football games on Friday nights instead of Friday afternoons.

You get the idea. The more relevant and timely—and sometimes, the more local—the more lively a debate you'll have, and the better illustration you'll make of this session's main point: how do you discern the truth when confronted by contradictory claims?

Invite two creative students to debate the chosen topic, or simply divide the group into two teams with each team making a case for its side of the question.

If two individuals debate, send them out of the room to prepare. Then ask the group—

- **What persuades you to believe one side or the other in a debate or argument?**
- **When someone's trying to prove something to you, what gives them credibility in your eyes?**

Jot down their answers on a whiteboard or overhead, then cover the answers and invite the debaters back into the room.

If your group divides in half for a groupwide debate, save these questions for the end. Just give each team 10 minutes to brainstorm its case.

Then each team presents arguments. If

individuals are debating, limit their arguments to, say, three minutes each followed by a one-minute response to the opponent's arguments. In the case of two teams debating each other, limit speakers to 30 to 60 seconds followed by a five-minute huddle for debriefing and prepping for the response. Give each side one minute to respond to the other team's arguments.

If you held a group debate, now is the time to ask the two questions stated above and record the group's answers. However you ran the debate, say something like—

Did anyone base an argument on a source outside of themselves? Scholars? Newspapers or other written sources? The opinion of someone with experience? Which argument convinced you? Why?

Bring into the discussion any of your students' comments from the whiteboard or overhead projector.

In the Book
[artsy-thinking option]

Storyboarding Paul's defense

stuff you'll need
- Bibles
- pencils or colored pencils
- a copy of **Storyboarding Paul's Defense** (page 26) for each group

Form small groups of three or four and distribute a copy of **Storyboarding Paul's Defense** (page 26) to each group. Have extra copies of the handout for groups who break the story into smaller pieces and need more frames. For younger students or groups that are already small, storyboard as a whole group and record your results on a whiteboard or overhead transparency.

Introduce the activity by saying something like—

Movie producers and interactive CD-ROM producers take the seed of an idea and a few notes, then draw out the flow of the action to see if they've got a story or not. In your small group, turn the storyboarding process upside down by first reading Paul's story as written in Galatians 1:11-2:10, and then recording it in sketches or words on your worksheet.

Upon completing your storyboard, use what you learned to summarize in a sentence how Paul's story might have given him credibility among the Galatian Christians.

When each small group has completed the activity, invite each group to offer its summary of how Paul's story might have given him credibility among the Galatian Christians. If students are willing, invite them to explain why they would believe that Paul's gospel is the true one—and by extension why they believe the Bible tells the true way to have a relationship with God. Invite those who are *not* sure they can believe Paul or the Bible to express why they have trouble believing.

In the Book
[small group Bible-snooping option]

The facts of the Galatian affair

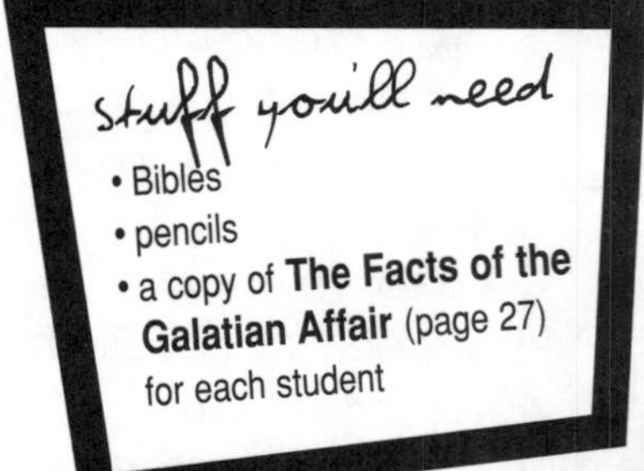
stuff you'll need
• Bibles
• pencils
• a copy of The Facts of the Galatian Affair (page 27) for each student

Say something like this—

Even if we're debating mundane matters like *Brushing and flossing my teeth is not worth getting up five minutes earlier to do*, we need to know the underlying facts of the issue. Who do we

believe? Who's telling us the truth about flossing—or about the value of college, or about how to live normally when your parents are divorced or divorcing? And at the bottom of it all, how do we know what's true about how God relates with us?

Here's the dilemma the new Christians in Galatia were struggling with: who was telling them the truth about God? The apostle Paul, who introduced them to the gospel of Christ, had said that faith in Jesus was the basis for their relationship with God. But he had no sooner left town than a group within the new church started teaching that faith in Jesus had to be accompanied by circumcision in order for God to accept their worship.

Who was right? Who should the church believe?

Form small groups of five to 10 people and give them pencils, Bibles, and **The Facts of the Galatian Affair** (page 27). Make sure they—or you—read the simple instructions at the top of the sheet.

- You can unveil the emotion of the letter by reading the passage to students from *The Message*, *The New Living Translation*, or another conversational English translation.

Debrief the small groups by asking them to return to the large group and share highlights of their answers and discussions. Conclude this section by asking the whole group to respond to the final question on the worksheet:

Do you think the credentials that Paul gave in the first third of his letter to the Galatians should have satisfied them that he was an authentic apostle and that the gospel he preached was the true one?

Guide responses to lead the group to discuss whether they accept Paul's message as the true gospel. Some will and some won't. Don't try to tie up their doubts and questions in a nice bow. Move to the closing.

Because this session's *Small group Bible-snooping option* is heavy with details and factual information, here are some explanations and suggested responses to the questions in **The Facts of the Galatian Affair**.

Galatians 1:6-10
Galatians 6:11-18

- *Describe Paul's mood as he writes this letter. What phrases in the reading clued you in to his mood?* Responses may include frustration (1:6), anger (1:9); or defensiveness (2:2). You'll unveil the emotion of the letter by reading the passage to students from *The Message* or another contemporary English translation.
- *What's happening in Galatia that's making Paul feel this way? Why is he writing to the Galatians, anyway?* Apparently the believers in Galatia had turned away from Paul's gospel of salvation by grace through faith in Jesus Christ—to embrace a message that said they must also be circumcised and obey the Law of Moses. He's writing to warn them off of that perversion of the true gospel.
- *What is the "different gospel" that Paul refers to in verse 6? What's the big deal about circumcision? Check back with Genesis 17:10-14, where God explains it to Abraham.* The big deal about circumcision, as the students discovered in session 1, is that the solemn sign of God's covenant with Israel was circumcision. And some Jewish converts to Christianity simply didn't get it—that God's point, even in ancient time, had been the

cutting away of the ungodliness of the heart—not merely cutting away the male foreskin. Compare Ezekiel 36:24-28.

Galatians 1:11-24; Acts 9:1-9

- *What point might Paul hope to make with the Galatians when he says he didn't receive the gospel from traditions or from schooling?* One point may be that the agitators in Galatia were saying he got his lessons wrong. To their way of thinking, it was a no-brainer that circumcision was required. Paul wanted the Galatians to know that the message hadn't come to him through schooling anyway, but straight from Jesus—so it wasn't *him* who was off base.
- *Where did Paul receive the gospel? How?* See Acts 9:1-9. Paul was confronted by the risen Christ and shown how much he must suffer for the name of Christ. He was then filled with the Holy Spirit. During that experience, and his subsequent time alone, he was taught by Jesus the meaning of the forgiveness of sins by grace through faith.
- *What was the result of Paul's conversion and revelation (Galatians 1:24)?* The result of Paul's conversion and revelation was that the Christian churches in Judea—the first churches formed after Christ's ascension—recognized Paul's gospel as authentic even though he hadn't consulted with any of them. And they worshiped God because God had turned the heart of a former persecutor to the gospel.

Galatians 2:1-10

- *After 14 years of preaching the gospel he'd learned from Jesus, Paul showed up in Jerusalem to meet with the other apostles. What was his purpose?* To tell them face to face about the revelation of the gospel he received from Christ. Perhaps he waited all that time so he would have fruit from his labor to demonstrate the truth of the gospel he preached.
- *What was significant about the person he brought with him to the meeting?* He introduced Peter, James, and John to Titus, an uncircumcised Gentile believer. Titus was living proof that the gospel of salvation by grace through faith produced godliness—apart from perfect obedience to the Law of Moses, including circumcision.
- *What didn't result from the meeting (Galatians 2:1-3)?* The other apostles didn't compel Titus, a Gentile believer, to be circumcised.
- *Who were three of the men Paul met with? What was the result of his meeting?* Peter, James, and John. These long-time leaders of the Christian church affirmed Paul's gospel.
- *Do you think the credentials that Paul gave in the first third of his letter to the Galatians should have satisfied them that he was an authentic apostle and that the gospel he preached was the true one?* Various responses will emerge, depending upon where students are in their experiences with evidences for the truth of the Christian faith.

Closing

When saying it is all you can do

stuff you'll need

- a copy of **A Couple of Creeds** (page 28) for each student
- **For a variation on this activity:** Rich Mullins' music CD called *A Liturgy, a Legacy & a Ragamuffin Band*

Say something like—

The phrase "I believe" has been misused so often that we've come to understand it to mean "I think" or "My opinion is."

Then when people ask if we believe in Jesus, we feel we've got to have studied enough to have our beliefs about him rock solid. Instead, simply a desire to worship is a significant form of belief to build on.

The way you build on that desire is to sing songs of worship and join in prayers and other Christian liturgies without requiring yourself to understand their full meaning. Repetition of words of faith, layered over your recent experiences, enlightens your sprouting belief. Writer Kathleen Norris puts it this way—

> **Over time, it was the ordinary events of life itself, coming "in between" the refrain of the church service, with its familiar creeds, hymns, psalms, and scripture stories, that most developed my religious faith. Worship summed it up and held it together, and it all made to seem like a [poem] to me, one that I was living.** —*Amazing Grace: A Vocabulary of Faith* (New York: Riverhead Books), p. 64.

Repeating a creed can affirm the aspects of the Christian faith handed down to you that you fully understand, and allow you to simply ride the tide of the faith of believers through the ages when you're struggling with doubt. In recognition of our connection with the faith of early Christians, we'll read together a creed that churches often recite during worship.

Or instead of reciting the creeds yourselves, you can invite your youth group to bow their heads and listen to Rich Mullins' "Creed" on his album *A Liturgy, a Legacy & a Ragamuffin Band.*

Storyboarding Paul's defense

- First, storyboard Paul's testimony from Galatians 1:1-2:10. Use words or pictures to show events and represent the timeline Paul describes. Get extra sheets if you need them.
- Next, summarize in a sentence how Paul's story might have given him credibility among the Galatian Christians. Be ready to share your summary with the whole group.
- Finally, discuss whether Paul convinced you that his gospel was the true gospel.

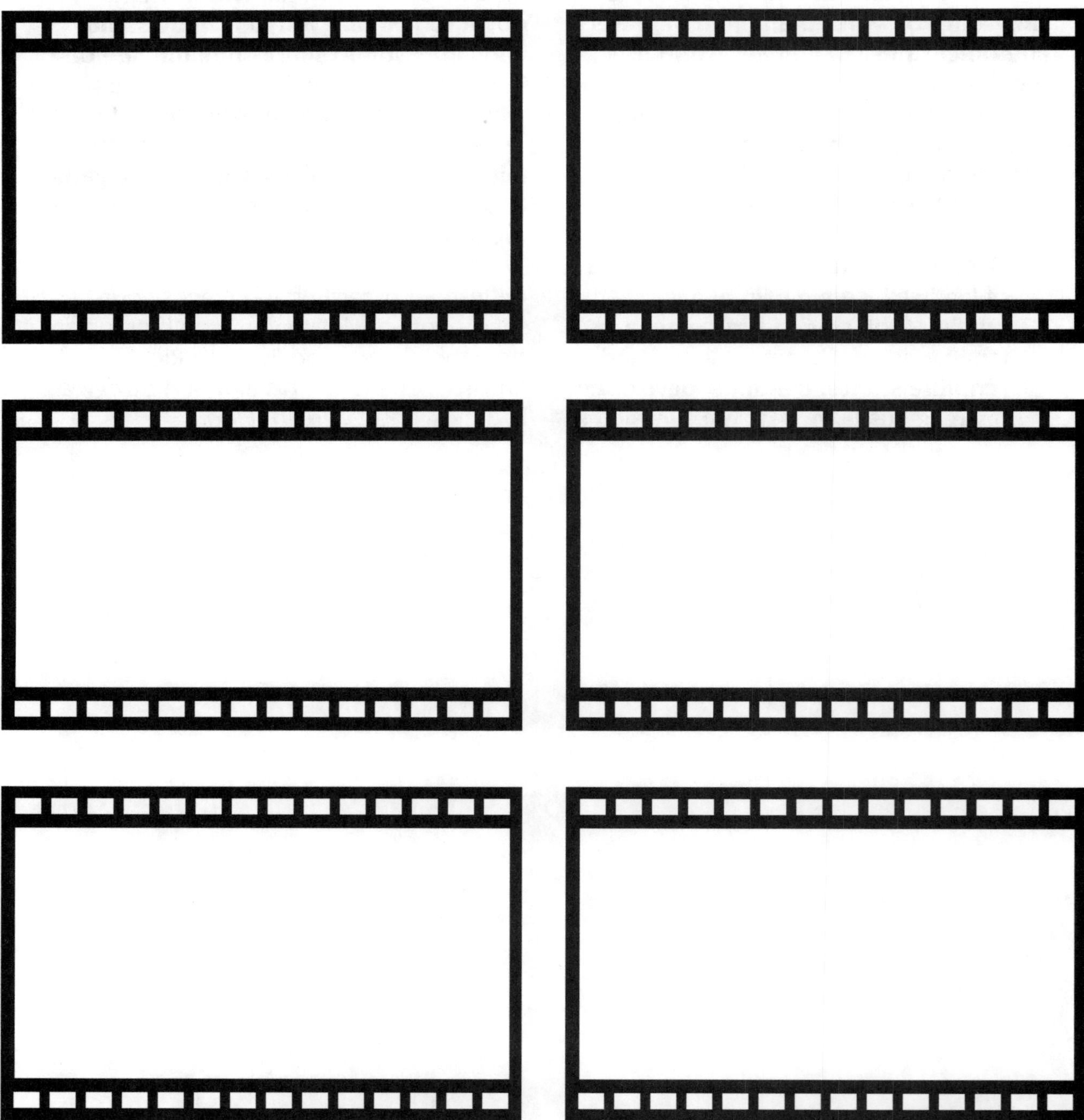

Write a sentence that tells how Paul's story convinced the Galatians that his gospel is the true gospel.

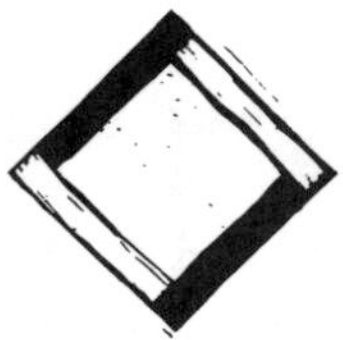

The facts of the Galatian affair

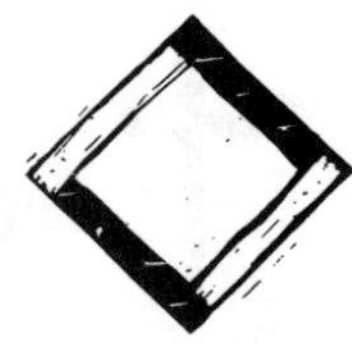

First, talk about this—
What issues are important enough to you that you would defend them passionately?

Now choose one of the following three sets of Bible verses to read. After reading the verses, talk about the questions or statements that follow. You may want to jot down some insights your group comes up with, or something memorable that one of you may say.

Galatians 1:6-10
Galatians 6:11-18

- Describe Paul's mood as he writes this letter. What phrases in the reading clued you into his mood?
- What's happening in Galatia that's making Paul feel this way? Why is he writing to the Galatians, anyway?
- What is the "different gospel" that Paul refers to in verse 6? What's the big deal about circumcision? (Check back with Genesis 17:10-14, where God explains it to Abraham.)

> Eugene Peterson's *The Message* translates verse 6 like this: "[A 'different gospel'] is not a minor variation, you know; it is completely other, an alien message, a no-message, a lie about God. Those who are provoking this agitation among you are turning the Message of Christ on its head."

Galatians 1:11-24

- What point might Paul hope to make with the Galatians when he says he didn't receive the gospel from traditions or from schooling?
- Where *did* Paul receive the gospel? How? (see Acts 9:1-9)
- What was the result of Paul's conversion and revelation (verse 24)?

Galatians 2:1-10

- After 14 years of preaching the gospel he'd learned from Jesus, Paul showed up in Jerusalem to meet with the other apostles. What was his purpose?
- What was significant about the person he brought with him to the meeting?
- What *didn't* result from the meeting? (verses 1-3)
- Who were three of the men Paul met with? What was the result of his meeting?
- Do you think the credentials that Paul gave in the first third of his letter to the Galatians should have satisfied them that he was an authentic apostle and that the gospel he preached was the true one?

Finally...

- Anything in these verses that's a puzzle to you? That just doesn't make sense?

- What one thing got your attention most of all in these verses? Why did it affect you the way it did?

† A couple of creeds †

The Nicene Creed

The Nicene Creed was written by the early Church and adopted in a slightly different version by the Church Council at Nicæa in A.D. 325. It appears in its present form by the Council at Chalcedon in A.D. 451. It has remained in use since that time.

We believe in one God,
the father, the Almighty,
maker of heaven and earth,
of all that is, seen and unseen.

We believe in one Lord, Jesus Christ,
the only Son of God,
eternally begotten of the Father,
God from God, Light from Light,
true God from true God,
begotten, not made,
of one Being with the Father;
through him all things were made.
For us and for our salvation
he came down from heaven,
was incarnate of the Holy Spirit and the Virgin Mary
and became truly human.
For our sake he was crucified under Pontius Pilate;
he suffered death and was buried.
On the third day he rose again
in accordance with the Scriptures;
he ascended into heaven
and is seated at the right hand of the Father.
He will come again in glory
to judge the living and the dead,
and his kingdom will have no end.

We believe in the holy Spirit, the Lord, the giver of life,
who proceeds from the Father and the Son,
who with the Father and the Son
is worshiped and glorified,
who has spoken through the prophets.

We believe in the one holy catholic and apostolic church.

We acknowledge one baptism for the forgiveness of sins.

We look for the resurrection of the dead,
and the life of the world to come. Amen

From *The United Methodist Hymnal*
(The United Methodist Publishing House, 1989), p. 880.

The Apostles' Creed, Traditional Version

This creed is called the Apostles' Creed not because it was produced by the apostles themselves, but because it contains a brief summary of their teachings. In its present form it is dated no later than the fourth century.

I believe in God the Father Almighty,
maker of heaven and earth;

And in Jesus Christ his only Son our Lord:
who was conceived by the Holy Spirit,
born of the Virgin Mary,
suffered under Pontius Pilate,
was crucified, dead, and buried;
the third day he rose from the dead;
he ascended into heaven,
and sitteth at the right hand
of God the Father Almighty;
from thence he shall come to judge
the quick and the dead.

I believe in the Holy Spirit,
the holy catholic church,
the communion of saints,
the forgiveness of sins,
the resurrection of the body,
and the life everlasting. Amen.

From *The United Methodist Hymnal*
(The United Methodist Publishing House, 1989), p. 881.

Session 3
The Great
Dinner-Seating
Fiasco—or
the Power of
Disapproval

Galatians 2:11-21
Galatians 5:1-12

During this session students will—

- Recognize in their culture temptations to heresy similar to the temptations posed by the Judaizers in Galatia.
- Feel indignation over hypocrisy, like Paul might have felt. Yet they'll practice tempering that indignation by extending grace to the offenders.

Paul models Christian freedom, then teaches it

We all love the idea of Christian freedom. Now ponder its hard edge: Paul didn't let Peter get away with undermining this freedom—a freedom from the constraints of Jewish law, a freedom that Paul knew Peter believed himself deep down inside.

Christian freedom is not only "what I can do"—sometimes it means *having* to do something. In Peter's case, Paul felt he *had* to confront Peter publicly in order for the Gentile Christians—including those in Galatia—to keep on living in the freedom given them by Jesus.

This week notice when you or Christians you know model this sometimes-unpleasant, sometimes-confrontational aspect of Christian freedom. You're bound to end up with illustrations to bring your lesson home where you and your students are. Christian love isn't always "nice," as Paul demonstrates.

Inform your teaching
Face-off at Antioch

If you had to name the heavy hitters in first-century Christian circles, Peter and Paul would be at the top of your list. Elsewhere in the New Testament these two apostles generally see eye to eye—but in his letter to the Galatians, Paul recounts how he publicly confronted Peter earlier in Antioch. It didn't turn into a slugfest, thank goodness—at least it is highly unlikely that the man who later wrote that God gives believers gifts of patience, joy, and peace would actually take a swing at another apostle.

In any case, Paul called Peter on the carpet for being a hypocrite. Apparently,

Peter had been mingling with the new Gentile (non-Jewish) converts in Antioch just fine, thank you. And this "mingling" was a huge thing. For millennia God had made it clear that in many ways, ritually and practically, Jews were *not* to mingle with non-Jews. Then Peter himself got the new message from God (Acts 10) that Jews are not superior to Gentiles. That Jewish rituals no longer determine one's standing with God. That animal sacrifices, the keeping of Jewish holy days, the abstention from certain foods, circumcision—to name just a few of many Jewish requirements—were not required to be a Christian.

There were two large cities named Antioch.

- Pisidian Antioch (in southern Galatia)
- Syrian Antioch (the Antioch of Acts 11, where Paul spent some time early in his Christian experience)

This Antioch of this dinner-seating fiasco was probably the latter.

When they first heard these words, the eyes of Jewish followers of Jesus got very, very wide. However much the Christian Jews loved Jesus, it wasn't an easy transition to try to share your life with—ick!—Gentiles. You don't just flush two thousand years of strict obedience to Yahweh down the toilet. You might as well have expected Selma, Alabama, to welcome blacks into mainstream white society as soon as the Civil Rights Bill was passed in the 1960s. It took a summit meeting of all the apostles in Jerusalem, including Peter and Paul, to agree that yes, non-Jewish converts were as welcome in God's family as Jewish converts—and no, they were not subject to Jewish customs. The grace that brought a Jew to Jesus also could bring a Gentile to him—and with no strings attached.

Remember that Christianity started off as a Jewish phenomenon. Jesus lived as a Jew, most of his disciples were Jews, the sacraments Jesus gave the church were undisguised extensions of Jewish rites, and the first gatherings of "Christians" were in synagogues.

The conservatives disapprove

Peter, aware of the full membership of Gentiles in the church, has been mingling with them during communal mealtimes—a common custom in the early church. But as soon as some suits from Jerusalem dropped in for a visit, Peter caught a bad case of peer pressure from them. Under the disapproving eyes of these conservative Jewish Christians, Peter made a public statement to the Gentile believers in Antioch without saying a word. After weeks or months of easily sitting among Gentiles during meals, he took his bowl and bread to a table of only Jews. The message to the new Gentile Christians was loud and clear: "Sorry, but I guess I'm not one with you after all. Gotta be a good Jew, you know. In fact, *you've* gotta be good Jews, too. Circumcision sign-ups are after dinner. Can't be a good Christian without being a good Jew, right?"

Hypocrites

Let's be clear about what a hypocrite is and isn't, what with all the "I don't go to church because of all the hypocrites there" excuses. Christians who don't behave as well as they want to are not hypocrites, but merely badly behaved—but hopefully growing—Christians. A hypocrite, on the other hand, is one who gives every impression of believing one thing, while privately believing something else entirely.

When Paul called Peter a hypocrite for separating himself from the Gentile Christians, it was a serious charge, but not without hope. Yes, Peter was a hypocrite, pretending to believe something he actually did not believe at all. But what was it he *really* believed? Peter was a hypocrite because he *actually believed* that Gentiles could come to Christ without first becoming good Jews—but under pressure he acted like he believed otherwise. (What would have been downright insidious is if Peter had actually believed in tying non-Jewish Christians to Jewish laws, but had pretended to be a big believer in Christian liberty.)

What made Paul go ballistic was that the Gentile Galatian Christians *believed* this perversion of the good news—even though Paul had spent time with them earlier, drilling into them the grace of

God, the uselessness of religious laws and rules to make anybody righteous. And then to watch Peter affirm that perversion by moving to the Jewish dinner table—well, Paul couldn't just let that pass unchallenged.

Grace has a sharp edge, too

The Great Dinner-Seating Fiasco also unsheaths the edge of grace. Face it, *grace* has an all-sweetness-and-light feeling—grace is free, grace is a gift, grace is effortless, grace looks right through my lousy behavior. This is all true. But like most truths, this one has two sides, and the other side of grace is this: you have to hold on tenaciously to grace, Paul writes, because there are those who will snatch it away in a heartbeat if they can.

But who would deny God's people his gift of grace? you ask. Answer: those who are suspicious and even fearful of grace and spiritual freedom. Because they don't trust themselves with such freedom—or often because they privately exploit or abuse their freedom—they don't let anyone under their influence have freedom.

Opener [game option]

Humanism 101

stuff you'll need

- both blue and yellow Post-Its
- the five **Humanism 101** quotes (pages 35-39) attached to the walls of the room
- tape or other temporary adhesive to attach the **Humanism 101** quotes to the walls
- enough slips cut from one or more photocopies of **What Do I Do with These Post-Its?** (page 40) so that each student has a slip

To prepare this opener, photocopy the five **Humanism 101** (pages 35-39) quotes. Then make enough copies of **What Do I Do with These Post-Its?** (page 40) to cut up and give one slip of instructions to each student. Post the quotes around the room before the students arrive.

As students come in, give each one two small pads of Post-Its—a yellow and a blue pad—as well as a **What Do I Do with These Post-Its?** slip. Tell them to read the instructions and take a few minutes to follow them before sitting down.

Here are the quotes:

- We are the creators of our future before us.
- What goes around comes around. Every good or evil deed we do comes back at us.
- Part of our task on earth is to end human cravings which are the source of wars and ecological disaster.
- All creation is one. In the end all blends together in the Unity.
- At the end of all things we can enter a state of complete freedom or emancipation if we live right.

from *The Perennial Dictionary of World Religions*

Debrief the exercise by saying something like—

Much of the substance abuse prevention, violence prevention, and environmental protection teaching in schools, workshops, and advertising media draws on the religious concepts of goodness, or being an enlightened individual, or being a faithful world citizen. Because it's easy to find parallels between other religions and Christianity, it's also easy for some Christians to absorb parts of these other religions into their understanding of Christianity.

Here are the fundamental religious concepts behind each of the quotes on the wall. (From *The Perennial Dictionary of World Religions*, HarperSanFrancisco, 1990.)

Quote: "We are the creators of our future before us."
Extension: The Buddha's teaching on the meaning and purpose of life—"We are the creators of our future before us. This is where our intentions come in. It is within our power to develop good deeds which will result in rebirth in a good state of existence, or to practice the religious discipline prescribed by the Buddha for breaking the bonds of rebirth."

Quote: "What goes around comes around. Every good or evil deed we do comes back at us."
Extension: Buddhist and Indian teaching of Karma (fruits of actions)—"Karma results from acts or deeds as well as the intentions behind those deeds, and represents the 'fruits' arising from those thoughts and actions. Every deed or thought produces karma which may be good or evil. According to the karma of the past, a living being will undergo repeated rebirths and assume a different form in each rebirth."

Quote: "Part of our task on earth is to end human cravings which are the source of wars and ecological disaster."
Extension: Buddhist teaching—"All existence is suffering. This universal suffering is brought about by craving for continual existence, sensual pleasure, fame, and power. Such cravings give rise to deeds that generate karma which in turn leads to further rebirth." And the cycle of suffering continues.

Quote: "All creation is one. In the end all blends together in the Unity."
Extension: Buddhist teaching—"There is no permanent self or soul. The true self of man is the universal self, and as soon as one realizes this unity, one becomes emancipated. The Buddha surveyed the world and found mankind attached to this self or soul, thinking it to be something eternal and permanent. Such a belief in the permanence of a self was held by the Buddha to be a pernicious error, as it gives rise to attachment, attachment lead so egoism, egoism begets craving for existence, fame, pleasure, and fortune, and this binds the individual to further rebirth and suffering."

Quote: "At the end of all things we can enter a state of complete freedom or emancipation if we live right."
Extension: Buddhist and Indian teaching on Nirvana—"By adhering strenuously to the regimen of moral conduct, mental discipline, and intuitive wisdom, which may stretch over numerous rebirths, the individual hopes to eradicate the craving that is the generating force behind all karma and repeated rebirth, and when he realizes this goal, he achieves emancipation or Nirvana."

Bottom line:
Christians who buy into the Buddhist or Indian or other religious philosophies that so subtly pervade our American scene are making the sacrifice of Christ merely a sideshow. These religious philosophies, like the perverted Judaism that Paul's opponents preached, depend on people changing themselves in order to get into right relationship with the Other, the Divine, or the Oneness. It throws those who follow those teachings into a system of keeping rules and working to please God—an undertaking that no one can successfully complete.

Listen to Paul himself explain it: "We [Jewish Christians] know very well that we are not set right with God by rule keeping but only through personal faith in Jesus Christ. How do we know? We tried it—and we had the best system of rules the world has ever seen! Convinced that no human being can please God by self-improvement, we believed in Jesus as the

Messiah so that we might be set right before God by trusting in the messiah, not by trying to be good." (Galatians 2, *The Message*)

Whether it's disapproving conservatives from Jerusalem or the latest entertainment and marketing messages, there's a lot of pressure on us to *not* live in line with what we believe—that God's grace through faith in Jesus Christ is what saves us, makes us whole, and fits us to live with God forever. We're offered an appealing platterful of alternatives. What will we choose?

Opener [tension-getter option]

How hyp are you?

stuff you'll need

- a copy of **How Hyp Are You?** (pages 41-42) for each student
- pencils

This opener sets up your students to understand the hypocrisy Peter was guilty of, when faced with the disapproval of visiting leaders.

Before you lead your students in this opener, you may first want to summarize or read verbatim the paragraph from **Inform your teaching** about what hypocrisy is and isn't.

Then move on to the activity with words like this to your students—

It's easy to get pressured into behaving differently than you really believe—in other words, to be a hypocrite. Take three minutes to decide how guilty of hypocrisy some people are.

And then distribute **How Hyp Are You?** (pages 41-42). If students resonate with the ambiguity of some of these scenarios, take some time to process the scenarios with your students.

In the Book
[guest-speaker option]

Boss Man Paul tells about his fight with Peter the Rock

stuff you'll need

- Two copies of the script for **Boss Man Paul Tells about his Fight with Peter the Rock** (page 43-44)

You'll need the help of another adult or a student to perform this interview with Paul about his confrontation of Peter in Antioch. Don't worry—this interview isn't nearly as rowdy as the SWWF panel in session 1!

In the Book
[small group Bible-snooping option]

Give me liberty, or give me dea—(hmmm...) is slavery still an option?

stuff you'll need

- Bibles
- pencils
- a copy of **Give Me Liberty, or Give Me Dea—hmmm...Is Slavery Still an Option?** (page 45) for each student

Before asking students to form groups of four or five, tell them they'll be reading a story that shows how passionately Paul defended a Christian's freedom from following rules as a path to God. Say something like—

The story you'll read in your small groups tells about the time one apostle, Paul, called another apostle, Peter, on the carpet—in front of the people Peter served and those in authority over him. It happened that the authorities came into town and saw Peter eating with non-Jews, which was a big no-no according to Jewish law. The authorities saw Peter's

action as meaning that Peter no longer observed the Mosaic fasts or taboos, and that he agreed with Paul that no Gentile Christian had to live like a Jew.

And it was true—Peter *did* agree with Paul. But after these authorities had done a few seminars around town, they actually got Peter feeling guilty enough to move to the other side of the room, refusing to be "defiled" or dirtied by eating with Gentiles.

What's the big deal about who you eat with, you ask? Well, the big deal was that it was just the tip of the iceberg of Jewish laws. And the conservative Jewish Christians were teaching that you weren't even a Christian if you didn't also obey all the Jewish laws—from who you eat with to circumcising all males. In other words, they taught that Jesus by himself can't redeem a person—that person has to redeem himself as well by obeying all 619 Jewish laws—without blowing it.

So you can see why Paul couldn't just shrug his shoulders and say, "Hey, it's only dinner," because it was so much more. Because it turned the gospel he had received from Jesus into a sideshow. And since Peter had publicly shown his hypocrisy, Paul had to publicly correct him. This could've been the end of Peter's ministry among the Gentiles. It could have confirmed the heresy that people have to follow rules to get to God. It was important.

Form small groups of five to 10 people and give them pencils, Bibles, and copies of **Give Me Liberty, or Give Me Dea—Hmmm...Is Slavery Still an Option?** (page 45). Make sure they—or you—read the simple instructions at the top of the sheet.

Closing

I have decided

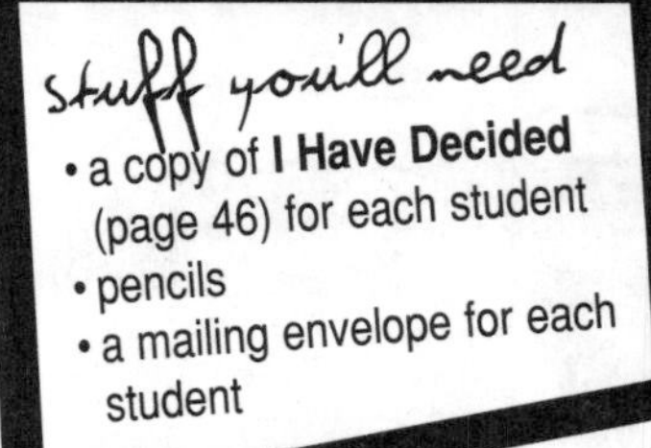
stuff you'll need
- a copy of **I Have Decided** (page 46) for each student
- pencils
- a mailing envelope for each student

Say something like—

Now it's time for you to think about a decision you need to make. Soon.

Give each student a copy of **I Have Decided** (page 46) and a blank mailing envelope. As the instructions say at the top of the sheet, students complete it with candid responses *for their eyes only*, seal it in the envelope, then address it to themselves. Collect the envelopes, assuring the kids that no one will read what's written unless they want them to. Wait two weeks, then mail the envelopes to them. You might want to jot on the back of the envelope something like "Have you stuck to your decision? If you want help, call me!"

We are the creators of our future before us.

What goes around comes around. Every good or evil deed we do comes back at us.

Part of our task on earth is to end human cravings which are the source of wars and ecological disaster.

All creation is one. In the end all blends together in the Unity.

At the end of all things we can enter a state of complete freedom or emancipation if we live right.

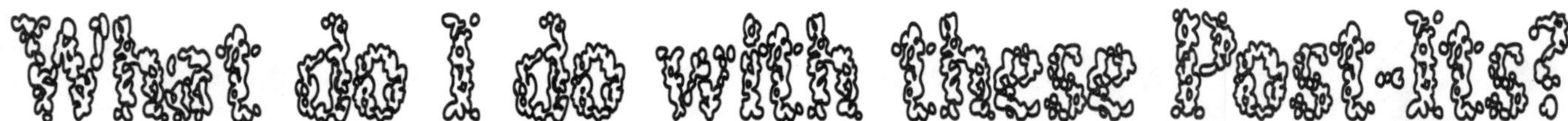

***Instructions to the youth leader**—Make enough copies of this page to cut into pieces so you can hand out one instruction slip to each student.*

What do I do with these Post-Its?

Posted around the room are quotes representing concepts you may be familiar with. Place a blue Post-It on any concept you recognize or have heard about. Place a yellow Post-It on any concept that seems to you to be true in some way—which means you could put one, both, or no Post-Its on a quote.

What do I do with these Post-Its?

Posted around the room are quotes representing concepts you may be familiar with. Place a blue Post-It on any concept you recognize or have heard about. Place a yellow Post-It on any concept that seems to you to be true in some way—which means you could put one, both, or no Post-Its on a quote.

What do I do with these Post-Its?

Posted around the room are quotes representing concepts you may be familiar with. Place a blue Post-It on any concept you recognize or have heard about. Place a yellow Post-It on any concept that seems to you to be true in some way—which means you could put one, both, or no Post-Its on a quote.

What do I do with these Post-Its?

Posted around the room are quotes representing concepts you may be familiar with. Place a blue Post-It on any concept you recognize or have heard about. Place a yellow Post-It on any concept that seems to you to be true in some way—which means you could put one, both, or no Post-Its on a quote.

What do I do with these Post-Its?

Posted around the room are quotes representing concepts you may be familiar with. Place a blue Post-It on any concept you recognize or have heard about. Place a yellow Post-It on any concept that seems to you to be true in some way—which means you could put one, both, or no Post-Its on a quote.

What do I do with these Post-Its?

Posted around the room are quotes representing concepts you may be familiar with. Place a blue Post-It on any concept you recognize or have heard about. Place a yellow Post-It on any concept that seems to you to be true in some way—which means you could put one, both, or no Post-Its on a quote.

What do I do with these Post-Its?

Posted around the room are quotes representing concepts you may be familiar with. Place a blue Post-It on any concept you recognize or have heard about. Place a yellow Post-It on any concept that seems to you to be true in some way—which means you could put one, both, or no Post-Its on a quote.

What do I do with these Post-Its?

Posted around the room are quotes representing concepts you may be familiar with. Place a blue Post-It on any concept you recognize or have heard about. Place a yellow Post-It on any concept that seems to you to be true in some way—which means you could put one, both, or no Post-Its on a quote.

How hyp are you?

Hypocritical, that is. Most people think hypocrisy is pretending to believe something you actually don't believe. But look at it inside-out: hypocrisy is also believing one thing, yet acting as if you believe something entirely different.

On a scale of 1 to 10, rate each of the following persons' Hypocrisy Quotient. Put a mark somewhere along the scale to indicate how hypocritical you feel that person is.

Molly

Molly's friend is pregnant. Molly believes abortion just isn't right—it seems like murder to her—but her friend's pain and rationalization gradually get Molly to reluctantly give her friend "permission" to get an abortion.

How hypocritical is Molly?

1————————5————————10

Not hypocritical at all — Official spokesperson for hypocrisy

Jesse

Jesse is already on the road with a family friend, headed toward a campground for a week's vacation, when he discovers that the friend likes disco. As in music. As in the BeeGees, Earth, Wind, and Fire, Gloria Gaynor, Donna Summer. As in Jesse begins dreading the week before it's begun. But he's been raised to be polite, so for the first couple of days he bites his tongue without dissing "Boogie Wonderland" and "Dancing Queen." The only problem is, the music kinda grows on Jesse. It's not that he exactly likes it, but by the end of the week, both the friend and Jesse are humming "YMCA."

How hypocritical is Jesse?

1————————5————————10

Not hypocritical at all — Official spokesperson for hypocrisy

Latisha

Latisha gets along pretty well with her parents—basically because they don't try to control every little event in her life. And when they do lay down the law, Latisha usually understands where they're coming from even though it bugs her now and then.

Yet when she's with her friend and conversation turns to parents, Latisha puts on this gripy attitude: "My parents are so picky...you wouldn't believe how they're all over me for the littlest things..."

How hypocritical is Latisha?

1————————5————————10

Not hypocritical at all — Official spokesperson for hypocrisy

Alano

Alano knows he's not ready for sex, wants to wait at least a while, maybe till marriage...who knows? But his new girlfriend really wants to have sex—and Alano really doesn't want to lose this girlfriend. This weekend he's planning to tell her that he's changed his mind.

How hypocritical is Alano?

1————————5————————10

Not hypocritical at all — Official spokesperson for hypocrisy

Trish

One night at Radio Shack a guy comes in while Trish is working and says he needs a data cable for his computer. She walks him to the wall display and points out the half-dozen different kinds of cables. The guy looks at them blankly.

"Look," he says, "I'm new at this. Which one should I get?"

Trish knows that her manager is trying to move the more expensive cables and that if she can sell even one or two during her shift, he'd notice it and appreciate it. She can also read specs and knows that the more expensive cables are no better than the cheaper ones, at least for this customer's application—in fact, she bought the cheaper cables for her own computer at home.

She reaches for one of the pricey data cables. "Here," she says. "This is what you want."

How hypocritical is Trish?

1 ———————— 5 ———————— 10

Not hypocritical at all — Official spokesperson for hypocrisy

Governor Kitzhaber of Oregon

(This is true.) The governor announces that he wants to use more of the state lottery income for treating gambling addictions.

How hypocritical is Governor Kitzhaber?

1 ———————— 5 ———————— 10

Not hypocritical at all — Official spokesperson for hypocrisy

Isabel

At the mall with a friend, Isabel sees a shirt in Nordstrom that is so garish and ugly they both can't help dissing it on the spot. Later that week at school, across the cafeteria, Isabel notices that the second most popular girl in school is wearing that exact same top.

A week later Isabel buys the shirt—and floors her friend, who asks her why oh why did she buy that shirt. "Oh, just changed my mind," she says.

How hypocritical is Isabel?

1 ———————— 5 ———————— 10

Not hypocritical at all — Official spokesperson for hypocrisy

Michael

Michael is a church youth worker who does his share of MP3 file trading—after all, he says, it isn't unfair to artists. MP3s give artists free exposure, and all the music files traveling around only increase the public's appetite for an artist's music—an appetite that most hearers will satisfy by buying the CD.

Yet Michael copyrights all his youth ministry lessons and preparation materials and attempts to sell them to Christian curriculum publishers.

How hypocritical is Michael?

1 ———————— 5 ———————— 10

Not hypocritical at all — Official spokesperson for hypocrisy

Dylan

In Dylan's opinion, welfare reform is long overdue. Living off a government handout only destroys one's initiative, he feels. Meanwhile, the 20-year-old is suing the high school he graduated from for failing to equip him to get a high-paying job.

How hypocritical is Dylan?

1 ———————— 5 ———————— 10

Not hypocritical at all — Official spokesperson for hypocrisy

Boss Man Paul tells about his fight with Peter the Rock

Cast
- Youth leader
- Paul

Youth leader: Earlier in our study of Galatians, Spiritual World Wrestlers Abraham Road Dog and Moses the Slasher came to our group to hype their upcoming fight over circumcision and the promise of God. The referee, Boss Man Paul, also showed up and surprised us with his outspoken bias toward Road Dog. He's back tonight to tell us about one of his own fights—a challenge against Peter the Rock.

Welcome, Paul. When did this fight take place?

Paul: A late summer night in '48. Barnabas, one of my roadies, and I made our way to Antioch after covering over a thousand miles on foot. All in about 60 days. We fought for the true gospel in city after city, and we have the scars to prove it.

Youth leader: So you and your gospel weren't well received?

Paul: Well now, I'd hate to put it that way, since God did so much in the lives of so many Gentiles—non-Jews, you know. But the Jews, now—my brothers—they're a feisty lot, resisting God's offer of salvation by faith in favor of useless attempts at keeping the whole Law of Moses.

Youth leader: So where does the Rock come into the picture?

Paul: Ah yes. Christians for miles around had come to Antioch in Syria to hear me and Barnabas talk about the victory of the gospel all over our world. Shoulder to shoulder we sat in the house-church there—no one caring that the smell of sweaty bodies was stronger than the stew. Jew and Gentile, rich and poor, slave and free—there was no difference among us.

Youth leader: I understand a contingent of conservative Jewish Christians joined the gathering later in the week?

Paul: That's when it happened. Up till that crowd showed, Peter ate with the mixed crowd without a flinch. It was he, you remember, who had the vision to go to Jews with the message that non-Jews were receiving God's salvation through Christ. But when those Slasher fans—those who call themselves The Circumcision—walked into the room, Peter lifted his coat over his head and eased on to a table by himself.

Youth leader: Now this happened during the so-called "love feast" that used to go on right before everyone ate the Lord's supper together.

Paul: That's right. You know, I was going to let it go, but then Barnabas sidled over to Peter. Barnabas—my right-hand man! The one who had waded in to fight for the gospel at every opportunity. That did it. I marched right over to Peter. I wasn't of a mind to deal with this quietly. By leaving the table where the uncircumcised Gentiles sat, he gave the strongest support possible to those who still believe a Gentile believer has to accept Jewish circumcision and Jewish laws about holy days and ceremonies or else he isn't really a Christian.

Youth leader: So Peter was influenced by the teachings of...

Paul: ...the teachings of these self-righteous, mutilating, wannabe Pharisees. "Peter, the Rock," I called out to him across the room. "You've been living like a Gentile all this while. You, a born and bred Jew." I didn't mince words. "But now that you think you'll look bad to these wannabes, you sit by yourself, as if to say you agree with these Christian Pharisees that believing in Jesus alone won't save you."

Youth leader: And that ticked him off.

Paul: No! That's the surprise ending for fight fans. He recognized his hypocrisy and changed his ways then and there.

Youth leader: I'd say that's more than a surprise—that's a disappointment. No fighting? No yelling back and forth across the room?

Paul: None. And Peter and I, out of all of us apostles, would have been most likely to resort to anger and violence. It's the Holy Spirit's work. I know it is. Both of us, we just—well, we're more into restoration and letting our faith in Jesus show itself through love.

Youth leader: Fight fans, you heard it with your own ears. Believe it or not. Big Boss Man and the Rock choose love and grace over laws and grudges. But we still have the big fight with the Slasher and Road Dog. There's bound to be some good action there. Y'all come back. Hear?

end

This script adapts information from John Pollock's book *The Apostle: A Life of Paul* (Chariot Victor Publishing, a division of Cook Communications, 1985).

Give me liberty, or give me dea— (hmmm...) is slavery still an option?

First, talk about this—
What have you thought was important enough to get in an argument with a friend?

Now choose one of the following three sets of Bible verses to read. After reading the verses, talk about the questions or statements that follow. You may want to jot down some insights your group comes up with, or something memorable that one of you may say.

Galatians 2:11-14

- Why does Paul bother arguing with Peter?
- What were Peter's options for responding to Paul's public reprimand of him?
- How would you feel about a friend prodding you to stand up for what they know you believe is right?

Galatians 5:1-6

- Standing firm (verse 1) is the opposite of tossing off a "Whatever." Paul is urging the Galatians to stay free and not go back into slavery. But what were they free from?
- What was the slavery they could return to?
- Why was Paul concerned with what they did? Wasn't it *their* lives they were messing with?
- Why does Paul say that becoming circumcised is a fall from grace?

Galatians 5:7-12

- Compare Paul's tone at this point in the letter with the tone he had in chapter 1.
- The Galatians had been running a good race, following the true gospel. Who cut in on them (verse 7)? How were they cut off? Cut off from what?
- Did it surprise you to read what Paul wrote in verse 12? Why or why not?
- Paul didn't get as worked up over other problems in the first-century churches he knew as he did against circumcision. He knew that some things were essential to the faith, while others were matters of personal preference. What do you think are the essentials of the Christian faith?

Finally...

- Anything in these verses that's a puzzle to you? That just doesn't make sense?
- What one thing got your attention most of all in these verses? Why did it affect you like it did?

I have decided

Write down your personal responses to these questions (your responses are *for your eyes only,* unless you wish otherwise), seal this page in the envelope, then address the envelope to yourself. It will be mailed to you in the near future to remind you to ask God's help in living by your decision.

In what area of your life are you feeling inclined to act in a way that doesn't reflect what you really believe?

☐ Relationship with parents
☐ Friendship choices
☐ School
☐ Dating decisions
☐ Extracurricular activities
☐ College/work
☐ Alcohol/drugs
☐ Other:

Who will hold you accountable to live what you really believe?

What kind of specific help can you ask God for in this matter?

I want to seek God's help in these ways (check one or more)—

☐ Reading the Scripture
☐ Finding out how other Christians have made a decision like this one
☐ Praying with a friend
☐ Praying alone
☐ Talking with a Christian friend I trust
☐ Talking with a pastor
☐ Talking with a parent
☐ Talking with a Christian adult I trust
☐ Other:

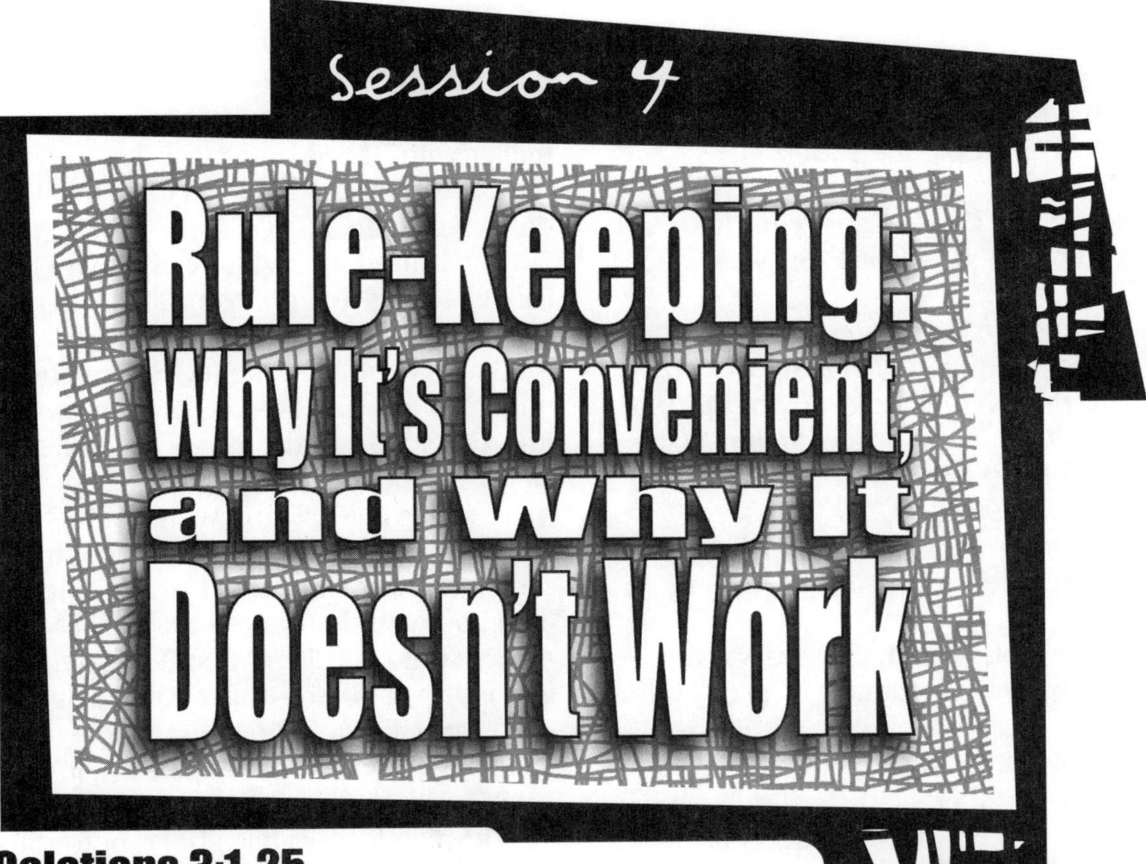

Session 4
Rule-Keeping:
Why It's Convenient,
and Why It
Doesn't Work

Galatians 3:1-25

During this session students will—

- Recognize that rules are meant to keep us in a path that will lead us to faith in Christ.
- Feel the tension between the freedom of coming to God by faith in Christ, and the need to guide their choices by the laws God has revealed under the guidance of godly leaders.

Inform your teaching

If it's good for the goose, it's good for the gander...or is it?

The premise of Paul's letter to the Galatians is this: the good news, the gospel of Jesus, is that we are saved by grace, not by keeping Moses' law...by a gift *to* us, not an effort *by* us.

But there's still good reason to follow the Law of Moses, Paul is quick to add.

Think of the law as a guardian, he wrote—a nanny, so to speak—who takes care of us until Christ comes. Before we knew God *through Jesus*, the best we could do was to follow God's laws as he gave them to Moses. But since Christ has come, we're not subject to the Law of Moses—we're free in Christ.

Woo-hoo! Par-tay!

Hold on a minute. Yes, salvation is now available *apart from the law*—namely, by grace. Still, Paul wrote, the law has a sacred place in the experience of Christ's

> **Why you do what you do**
>
> This week, notice and list whatever disciplines or rules you follow—rules that keep your soul on a safe path. Which ones are personal and, however strongly you feel about them, rules you don't expect other Christians to follow? On the other hand, which rules are pretty cut-and-dried as far as you're concerned—true for you because they apply to everyone?

church. Even Jesus said that he came to fulfill the law, not to abolish it (Matthew 5:17). Which stops one short of tossing the Torah, because there's still a place for Moses' law in God's plan for us. And Paul up and says it in Galatians 3:23-25:

> *Before this faith came, we were held prisoners by the law, locked up until faith should be revealed. So the law was put in charge to lead us to Christ that we might be justified by faith. Now that faith has come, we are no longer under the supervision of the law.*

And there you have it: the law was a supervisor until we came of age in Christ.

Two extremes of truth

A person can take this truth, as they can take any truth, and do exactly what Jesus *doesn't* want:

- Exploit and abuse the truth of our freedom in Christ, or
- Enforce this truth on *all* Christians.

Either extreme is just plain wrong—nowhere near what a simple reading of this letter shows is Paul's main point. Most of us have heard our share of sermons on one of these extremes—sermons that rein us in, that aim to dissuade us from using our freedom in Christ to live as if every day is Mardi Gras.

What we hear *less* often is how, sometimes, the same truth can look different on different Christians. Paul himself warned the churches in Rome (chapter 14) and in Corinth (chapters 7-8) about this quirk when it came to marriage, food, and circumcision. In other words, sometimes biblical truth means discovering what God wants *you* to do, then doing it—without thinking that it's God's will for *everybody.*

It seems like a universal tendency for us to define spirituality for *everyone* by the lifestyle that works best for *our* spiritual growth. This is an especially seductive temptation among persons in spiritual or ministry leadership.

The same thing was going on when Paul wrote his letter to the Galatians. Because of their covenant with God as mediated by Moses, the Jews were committed to obeying the law. As with most rule-keeping systems, more rules were gradually added to clarify the original rules. If God said, "Don't work on the Sabbath," then some leaders taught the people, "This means don't walk further than you would have to walk to pull your donkey out of a ditch." Or "Don't start a fire on the Sabbath—that's work. Just keep Sabbath Eve's fire going." Or "Cooking is work. On the Sabbath, just eat cold food." And so on.

Christian leaders have been notorious for doing just that to teenagers. Meaning well, said leaders want to keep kids on the paths of righteousness—so they legislate minutia. And kids respond the same way the Jews did—they dutifully obey all the jots and tittles their elders dictate for them, and in the course of toeing a spiritual line that Jesus never intended them to toe, they lose sight of Emmanuel, God with us. Or else they rationalize their disobedience of the synthetic rules and gradually lose the capacity to discern these man-made rules from God's original (and usually simpler) rules. Then they simply rationalize their way through *all* rules regarding their spiritual life—true rules as well as bogus rules.

Teenagers deserve better from us. Life is difficult, life is complex, and kids see right through us when we tell them otherwise. By the same token, Christ is merciful, Christ promises to walk with us through all the difficulty and complexity. And if we take a stab at living as though this is true, kids will again see right through us—but see Jesus, this time.

Opener [ethics/opinion option]

Decisions, decisions

stuff you'll need

- Just you, your group, and the instructions below

You could say this activity offers visible, kinetic translations of each person's ethical priorities—plus it gets your students thinking specifically about how we temper freedom with rules.

The instructions in one sentence: after you read the each statement below, students indicate their responses by moving one way or another about the room. Start by say something like—

I'm going to describe a situation and then ask you to walk—

- **to one side of the room if you make one particular choice,**
- **to the other side if you make the opposite choice, or**
- **to the middle of the room if you're not sure.**

I'll wait until you all make your move before giving you further details—circumstances that might make you rethink your decision. If those details cause you to change your mind, you can move to the place in the room that reflects your new decision.

During the activity, notice when people change their minds.

Ready? Everybody in the middle of the room? Okay, first situation:

- **You've just learned how to print a fake report card from your computer—right after failing math for the semester. Do you print one or not? (If you print, move to the side of the room to my left. If you don't print, move to my right. If you're not sure, stay in the middle.)**

Further details:

—What if you know your parents will find out what you did two years from now—say, when you're in college? *(Anyone who changes his mind may move now.)*
—What if your mom is best friends with your teacher? *(Anyone who changes her mind may move now.)*

- **You look over and see someone cheating on an English test. Do you tell or not?**

Further details:

—What if it's your boyfriend or girlfriend?
—What if the cheater will mess up the curve?

- **Your friend calls you at 1 a.m. He's been drinking and needs a ride home but doesn't want to call his parents. Do you drive him or not?**

Further details:

—What if you don't have a license?
—What if you think he might be an alcoholic?
—What if he or she is the opposite sex?

- **You've got tickets to see____________** [fill in the blank with the name of some primo show or concert], **but you're supposed to work the evening shift at The Gap. Your boss is very strict about employees keeping their work schedules. Do you call in sick or not?**

Further details:

—What if you're quitting in two weeks?

—What if your boss skips work sometimes?

- **One of your friends has a crush on someone, but that person asks *you* out. It's someone you're kind of interested in. Do you go out with your friend's crush?**

Further details:

—What if you know it would end your friendship?

—What if this person had already broken up with you before?

- **Someone asks you to donate money for____________** [name a local cause, or one that your kids may be sympathetic toward]. **You're almost broke and really want to go to a movie. Would you give your money to the charity?**

Further details:

—What if the charity is for dying children?

—What if you have a relative who'd benefit from the charity?

- **Someone asks you to move out of your house, drop out of school, and live in a homeless shelter to help feed the poor. Would you?**

Further details:

—What if you could finish school later?

—What if Jesus asked you?

Debrief the activity by recalling some of those changes. Lead the group to discuss them by saying—

Some of you who changed your mind about____________ *[read that situation again]***—would you tell why your decision first seemed right and then not right?**

Opener [humorous option]

Wicked Wanda

stuff you'll need

- a copy of **The Fairy Tale of Wicked Wanda** (pages 53-54) for someone to read from
- a narrator (you, maybe?) and at least eight impromptu actors
- a bag of Gummi Worms
- soda crackers

This is a *spontaneous melodrama*—one of those hilarious, boisterous, no-rehearsal, slap-sticky skits that get kids involved—whether they're hamming up front as impromptu actors or sitting in the audience cheering for the good guys, hissing the bad guys, and getting nearly as animated as the onstage actors. It's also an effective (albeit goofy) introduction to a biblical point.

Here's how to get the most mileage out of a spontaneous melodrama. Get your actors up front, assign them their parts (animate or inanimate), and tell them to do whatever you read in a broad, hammy way. When you read, "And the frog croaked, 'Okay, have it your way'—and promptly fell over dead," the croakier the student frog's voice as he repeats the line, and the more outlandish his falling over and twitching in his death throes, the better.

First read through **The Fairy Tale of Wicked Wanda** (pages 53-54) so you have a feel for the script. Recruit at least eight students and move them to center stage as part of the cast of this spontaneous melodrama—though you can use up to six students each for the parts of Whistleberry Bushes and Warbling Wrens.

Instruct your actors to this effect—

I'll narrate the spontaneous melodrama.

When in the story I describe something your character is doing, you act it out. If I read that you say something, you say it. If I read that you *do* something, you do it. Be outlandish and big and bold. Ready?

Then start the script.

In the Book
[observation & interpretation option]

What's really happening here? Galatians 3:15-29

stuff you'll need
- Bibles
- pencils
- a copy of **What's *Really* Happening Here? Galatians 3:15-29** (pages 55-56) for each student
- a couple sets of colored pencils per group
- if at all possible, an adult facilitator for each small group (not to steer kids into the "right" answers, but to clarify and possibly exemplify the steps in this Bible study)

Paul wrote Galatians, scholars say, in the same formal and highly structured style that legal cases were argued in Roman courts—tight, well-reasoned, and persuasive, with anecdotes that illustrate and support one's argument. Chapter 3, verses 15-29 is one piece of Paul's argument in Galatians.

Students ready to attempt the study skills of *observation* and *interpretation* can use **What's *Really* Happening Here? Galatians 3:15-29** (pages 55-56) to note repeated words, cross-references, and the train of Paul's argument. This works best if there is an adult facilitator with the group. Be sure you or the adult facilitators at least skim this handout yourselves so you can explain it to and possibly adapt it for your students.

In the Book
[small group Bible-snooping option]

Answering the Galatians' mail

stuff you'll need
- Bibles
- pencils
- copies of **Answering the Galatians' Mail** (page 57)

Hand out copies of **Answering the Galatians' Mail** (page 57) and ask students to form groups of four or five after your explanation. Say something like—

It's a no-brainer that there are certain rules you should follow—even if you have a high level of freedom. Driving, for example, brings a freedom that most kids long to enjoy. That freedom remains freeing only when people on the roads follow the rules of the road. It's obvious that otherwise that freedom brings suffering and death.

Paul was walking a line between legalism and libertarianism when he wrote Galatians. Yes we're free in Christ—free from the bondage of trying to obey rules in order to get in good with God. No, the rules—in particular Moses' law—couldn't give life the way faith in Christ could—but on the other hand, it served a good purpose in keeping Jews going in the right direction until Christ could come. This is true for all believers—that obeying the laws God gave to Israel keeps us in the path while Christ is being formed in us. You don't always have instant change in all of your bad behavior the minute you receive Christ. Instead, counting on the Holy Spirit who has made you new, you stay within the rules given by God and parents and godly leaders until you grow up in Christ and become skilled at making wise choices.

In your small groups, talk about how you would answer the questions about freedom and law that Paul asked the Galatians.

Take time after the small groups meet to discuss some of the highlights of their discussions.

Closing

Litany of grace

stuff you'll need

- one copy of **Litany of Grace** (page 58) for the leader to read

Tell the students you'll read a series of phrases. After each phrase they are to respond by saying, "His love endures forever." This litany is based on Psalm 136. Let this be your closing prayer. If you want it celebrative, have everyone shout the final *Amen!* If you want a more devotional mood, consider dismissing the meeting in silence after the *Amen*. Your call.

The fairy tale of Wicked Wanda

A spontaneous melodrama

Cast

- Narrator
- Wicked Wanda
- Whistleberry Bushes (two to six students)
- Warbling Wrens (two to six students)
- Wolf
- Wildebeest (WILL-deh-beest)
- Woodsman

Give a handful of Gummi Worms to the Warbling Wrens (they'll need them to feed to Wicked Wanda) and a couple to the Woodsman.

Narrator: Once upon a time, Wicked Wanda went for a walk. She waddled along the wide walkway. "This path is way too safe," Wicked Wanda whined. (In fact, she couldn't talk without whining.) "I wanna get away to some more interesting path." So she wandered far from her original path—she walked in circles—she walked in figure eights—she walked in spirals—always finding a new path and taking it.

"Ooh, what about that path over there?" she wondered aloud. And so Wicked Wanda whisked herself whimsically onto the new path—and deeper into the woods. Little did Wicked Wanda know that by wavering from the walkway, she would wind up getting wrapped in some wet whistleberry bushes filled with Warbling Wrens. The nearsighted birds fluttered around until they flew right into Wicked Wanda and fell to the ground, stunned. Then up they flew again, convinced they had to feed this big chick (who was still caught in the wet whistleberry bushes). So they stuffed Wicked Wanda's mouth with worms until her cheeks were filled with worms, and worms hung out of her mouth. Then the Wrens warbled this warning: "It's way wiser not to wander, but to return to the walkway."

Said Wicked Wanda in a whisper that could be heard for miles, "I will *not* go back to the wide walkway. It might be wiser, but it sure isn't as whimsical."

Suddenly, without warning, a wild wolf came woofing out of the woods.

"Woof!" woofed the wolf with a furry voice.

"Woof yourself," whined Wicked Wanda. "Don't waste my weekend with your wagging tongue, you wacko."

The wolf said, "I wasn't planning on wolfing you down. But now that I see you're such a wise guy, I think I just got hungry again. Here, fatten yourself up before I set the table." And the wolf fed Wicked Wanda soda crackers until she said, "Enough already!" Then, just to see if she could do it, she whistled the first few bars of "Our God Is an Awesome God." The Wolf said, "Enough already! Okay, I won't wolf you down, but remember this: Whenever we wander, it's wiser to return to the walkway."

Wicked Wanda wondered about the wisdom of this. She said, "Oh, I wish my wrongdoing wouldn't weigh on me," and she started to cry, loudly and continuously—as she pulled out her hair—as she fell down, pounding the ground with her fists and kicking, saying "I am such a worthlessly Wicked Wanda woman." Then she got up, straightened her hair, and said, "Well, maybe not all *that* bad."

At that instant, along walked a wandering Wildebeest, who whisked Wanda up on his back and bounded away, right through the wet whistleberry bushes, scattering the bushes every which way. "What in the world?" wailed Wicked Wanda to the Wildebeest. "Now I'll never find my way!" Then the Wildebeest dumped Wicked Wanda into the wet whistleberry bushes. Wicked Wanda said in her whiny-as-usual voice, "Not again!" The Wildebeest said, "Won't you ever learn? Whenever we wander, it's wiser to return to the walkway," then turned and disappeared from sight.

"Sounds familiar," said Wicked Wanda. "But look at me now. Whatever I do won't get me back to the walkway! My life's a waste! I'm a wreck!" Warbling Wrens that flew by saw her and had pity, so they dropped some worms for her out of their mouths. She ate a few to satisfy her appetite, and went to sleep. And started snoring. Finally she snored so loudly she woke herself up. And there next to her stood a Woodsman, who said, "I am here to answer an important need in your life." Then the Woodsman knelt before Wicked Wanda, looked wonderingly at her mouth, and said, "I can take care of those adenoids, you know. I mean, you're keeping the entire forest awake with your snoring."

Wicked Wanda leaped to her feet and shouted, "Don't talk to me about my adenoids, when I've wandered from the way, I'm almost wolfed by a Wolf, I'm wounded by whistleberry bushes, I'm abandoned by a wandering Wildebeest—look, I've got some big problems in my life, and snoring's not one of them." And she plopped down on the ground, and stuck out her lower lip in a big pout. Then she stuck her tongue out at the Woodsman. Then she tried to touch her nose with her tongue.

Said the Woodsman, "Yeccchh—if you stop that, I will take you to the right way again, okay?"

"You mean you know the way back?" Wicked Wanda asked.

"Yup," said the Woodsman. "But you've got to trust me."

To which Wicked Wanda replied, "Trusting isn't easy for me, you know."

"That's okay," said the Woodsman. "Just do your best to follow me, and we'll eventually get back to the way.

"Yowsa!" yelled Wicked Wanda. "If you can do that, I won't whine anymore! And neither will I wander!"

"Let's go then," said the Woodsman. "Hey, you hungry? I've got some worms here."

And with that, the Woodsman and Wicked Wanda wandered away, waiting and watching for a wondrous way to the path she first walked.

What's really happening here?

Galatians 3:15-29

First, read straight through this passage aloud—

15 Brothers, let me take an example from everyday life. Just as no one
can set aside or add to a human covenant that has been duly established, so
it is in this case. 16 The promises were spoken to Abraham and to his seed. [Genesis 12 and 15]
The Scripture does not say "and to seeds," meaning many people, but "and
to your seed," meaning one person, who is Christ. 17 What I mean is this: The [Gen. 12:7; 13:15; 24:7]
law, introduced 430 years later, does not set aside the covenant previously [Exodus 19-24]
established by God and thus do away with the promise. 18 For if the inheritance depends on the law, then it no longer depends on a promise; but God
in his grace gave it to Abraham through a promise.

19 What, then, was the purpose of the law? It was added because of
transgressions until the Seed to whom the promise referred had come. The
law was put into effect through angels by a mediator. 20 A mediator, however,
does not represent just one party; but God is one.

21 Is the law, therefore, opposed to the promises of God? Absolutely
not! For if a law had been given that could impart life, then righteousness
would certainly have come by the law. 22 But the Scripture declares that the [Psalm 14:1-3]
whole world is a prisoner of sin, so that what was promised, being given
through faith in Jesus Christ, might be given to those who believe.

23 Before this faith came, we were held prisoners by the law, locked
up until faith should be revealed. 24 So the law was put in charge to lead us
to Christ [or *in charge until Christ came*] that we might be justified by faith. 25
Now that faith has come, we are no longer under the supervision of the law.

26 You are all sons of God through faith in Christ Jesus, 27 for all of you
who were baptized into Christ have clothed yourselves with Christ. 28 There is
neither Jew nor Greek, slave nor free, male nor female, for you are all one in
Christ Jesus. 29 If you belong to Christ, then you are Abraham's seed, and
heirs according to the promise.

Now do this—

- Pray and ask God to give you understanding of this Scripture passage.

- Mark significant words that show up more than once with a unique symbol. For instance, a form of *promise* shows up several times. Mark it with a symbol—circle it, square it, sunburst it, draw a heart, cross, or other symbol on top of the word. You get the idea. You'll want to skim through the verses a few times to do this. But *don't start this yet,* because there's more.

- Choose a distinctive color for that word's symbol, too, so your eye can readily pick up a theme. Use a different color for each word symbol.

  When you come across the following words, mark each group of them as if they were the same word (because actually they're synonymous in these verses):
  – Mark all forms of the words *promise, covenant,* and *inheritance* with the same color.
  – Mark all forms of *seeds, heirs,* and *sons* with the same color.
  – Mark all forms of *faith, grace,* and *believe* with the same color.

- Okay, enough of the detail work. What two or three symbols or marks show up the most? When you cross your eyes and make the paper look blurry—a Bible study method not recommended by optometrists—what *colors* stand out the most? The marks and the colors that most catch your attention are often the themes of the Bible passage you're observing. So what's the theme of *this* passage?

- Who is Abraham's seed? (The answer is in one of the cross-references.)

- Explain who else Paul considers to be heir of the promise along with the seed of Abraham.

- What problem does Paul address in these verses?

- Summarize Paul's argument in your own words.

Answering the Galatians' mail

First, talk about this—
It's a no-brainer that there are certain rules you should follow—even if you have a high level of freedom. Driving, for example, brings a freedom that most kids long to enjoy. That freedom remains freeing only when people on the roads follow the rules of the road. It's obvious that otherwise that freedom brings suffering and death.

Question: what have you learned so far in your life experience that tells you that freedom stays free only when the free follow wise rules?

Paul asks the Galatians numerous questions in chapter 3. In your small group, take a shot at answering some of them. Put a check beside questions you think are dumb (like when your teacher yells at you and asks, "Do you just want to flunk out and spend what remains of your short and miserable life living under a bridge?"). But try to answer the questions that are valid to you, even if they seem personal. If you're not comfortable responding in the group, think through the answer just for your own understanding.

- How did your new life begin? To what extent did you work your head off to please God, and to what extent did you just let grace flow in around you?

- Is it hard to imagine a God who lavishly provides you with his own presence, his Holy Sprit—a God who works things in your life that you could never do for yourself? Or is it easier for you to imagine a God who does good things for you only because you're earning them with your good, clean living?

Galatians 3:15-20

- What promises did God speak to Abraham? See Genesis 13:14-16, Genesis 17:2-8, and Galatians 3:9.
- Who is Abraham's seed?
- Does the law invalidate the promises spoken to Abraham? Why not?

Galatians 3:21-25

- Could the law have made us righteous? Why or why not?
- What do you think Paul was imagining when he wrote about a world "imprisoned by sin"?
- Why did God give us commandments to follow?
- Why do we need the law?

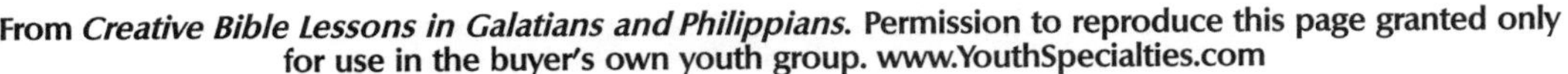

LITANY OF GRACE

(BASED ON PSALM 136)

Ask students to repeat "His loves endures forever" after each line you read.

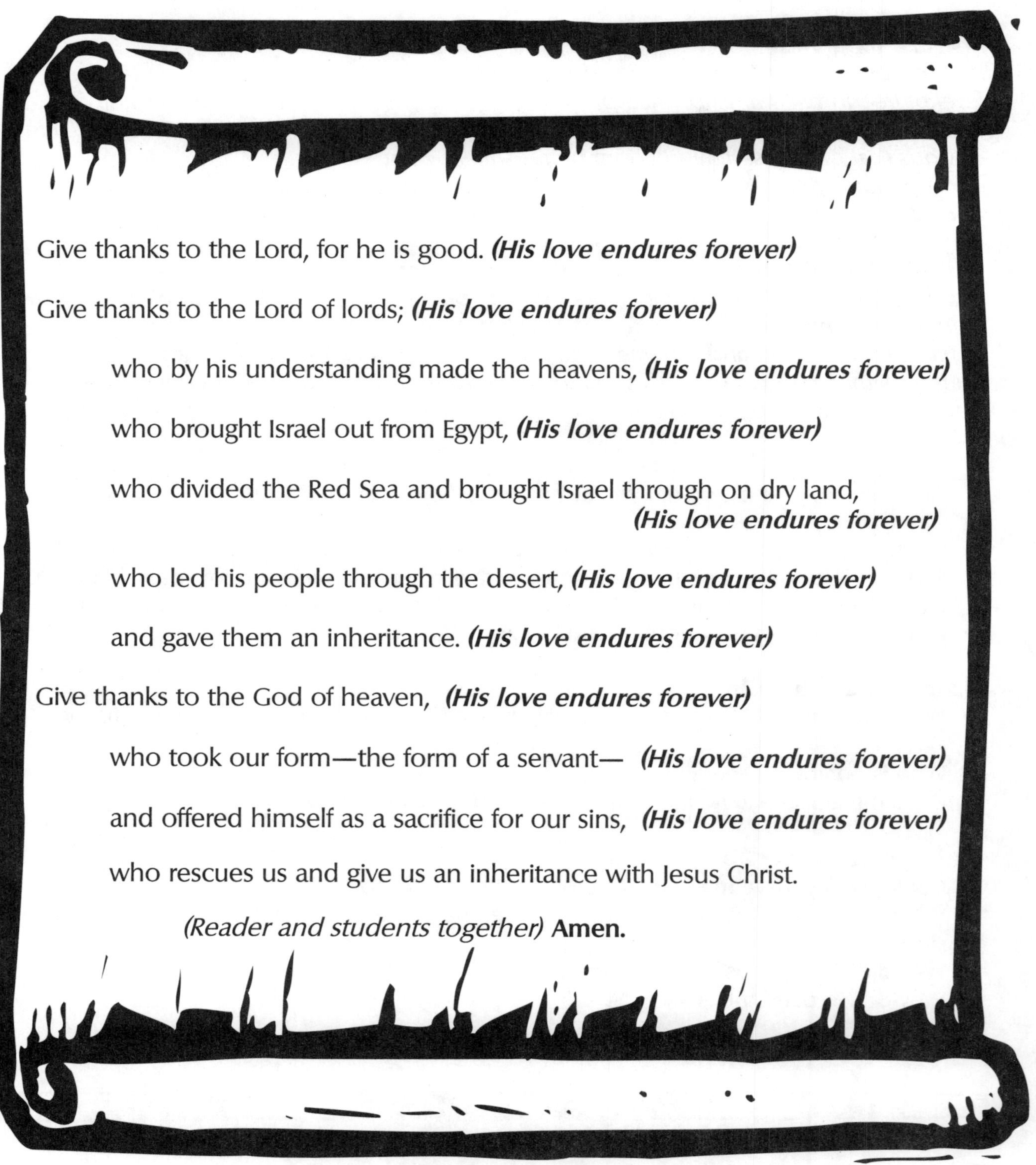

Give thanks to the Lord, for he is good. ***(His love endures forever)***

Give thanks to the Lord of lords; ***(His love endures forever)***

who by his understanding made the heavens, ***(His love endures forever)***

who brought Israel out from Egypt, ***(His love endures forever)***

who divided the Red Sea and brought Israel through on dry land, ***(His love endures forever)***

who led his people through the desert, ***(His love endures forever)***

and gave them an inheritance. ***(His love endures forever)***

Give thanks to the God of heaven, ***(His love endures forever)***

who took our form—the form of a servant— ***(His love endures forever)***

and offered himself as a sacrifice for our sins, ***(His love endures forever)***

who rescues us and give us an inheritance with Jesus Christ.

(Reader and students together) **Amen.**

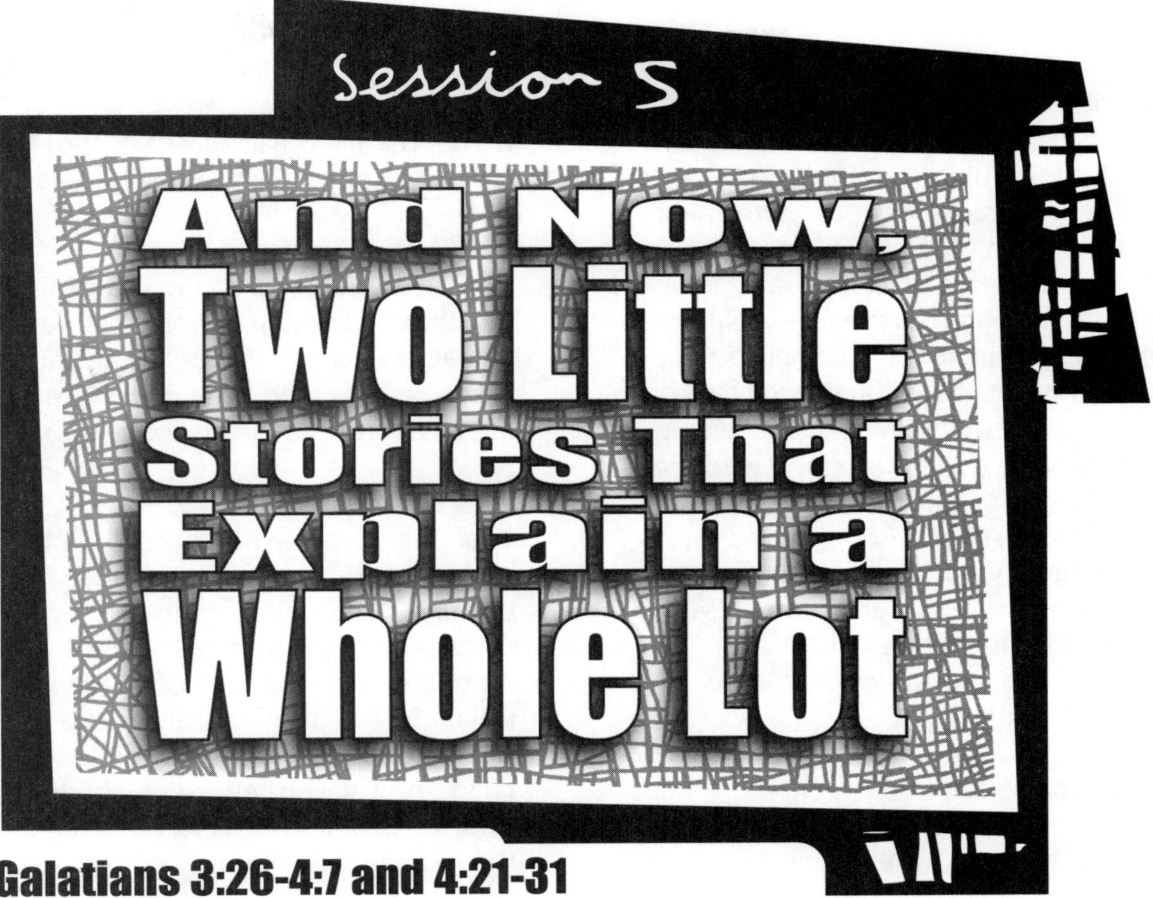

Session 5
And Now, Two Little Stories That Explain a Whole Lot

3:26-4:10 What/When can you apply this?

Galatians 3:26-4:7 and 4:21-31

During this session students will—

- Recognize that their faith gives them a new identity as a child of God—and an inheritance to go with it.
- Feel affirmed as capable of being led by the Holy Spirit to grow in Christian maturity.

Galatians points to Genesis—so guess what you should review?

Because Paul assumed that his Galatian readers were familiar with classic Genesis accounts, if you aren't, brush up on the promised-son dialogues and events in Genesis chapters 12, 15-18, and 21. It's actually quite a roller coaster ride—the stuff novels are made from. In fact, two novelists you should be reading have done exactly that—based novels on stories in Genesis: Frederick Buechner's *The Son of Laughter* (HarperSanFrancisco) about Isaac, and Walter Wangerin Jr.'s *The Book of God*, actually a novelization of the entire Bible that begins with—guess what—Abraham and Sarah's childlessness. Also relevant to all things Pauline is Wangerin's *Paul: A Novel* (Zondervan).

Okay, there's your reading list for the next year.

Inform your teaching

Defeating the legalists on their own legal ground

Seldom in his New Testament letters is the apostle Paul as systematic as he is in these passages. No, more than systematic—*ruthlessly logical*. And what's particularly excruciating about it is that, like a veteran courtroom attorney, he conducts his argument *on the defendants' turf*.

The defendants, you remember, are those Gentile believers in Galatia who were convinced by some legalistic Christians that like the Jews, the non-Jewish Christians had to obey the law. (That would be "the law of Moses," in general the first five books of the Bible, which contains stories and genealogies as well as the details of Jewish laws and rituals that God required of them.) In particular, the Gentiles had been taught they had to obey the Jewish law of circumcision. If the Jews had to do this in order to gain right standing before God, then who were the Gentiles to think they could sneak into God's good graces without performing this God-given rite?

Of course, this teaching—as traditional and time-honored as it was—was in absolute contradiction to what Paul had taught them earlier—that since Jesus had come and died and lived again, keeping the Mosaic law was about as useful for attaining righteousness as keeping back issues of *Christianity Today*. Good things that admirably served their purpose once and have now been surpassed by *better* things—the unconditional grace of God through Jesus and the current issues of *CT*, respectively.

Uh-one and uh-two and...

To drive his point home—and the wandering Galatians back into their true fold—Paul uses examples from the Torah. Paul's argument in this session's Bible passages runs like this, loosely:

1. There are no distinctions between believers in Christ. Before Jesus came on the scene it used to matter if one was a Jew or a Gentile (non-Jew), but no more. The attempted distinctions may go beyond ethnic Jew-Gentile differences, to sexual or socioeconomic differences. It didn't matter, Paul told the Galatians—however people try to divide you diverse Christians up, resist it. Because you're all one in Jesus Christ now.

2. There's more. Not only *aren't* Gentiles second-class Christians compared to Jewish Christians, but Gentile believers have as much right to call Abraham their father as Jews do.

3. Here's how. God promises Abraham a son. Yet Abraham knows his wife is barren. To give her husband the son he needs, Sarah willingly gives him her slave Hagar (just for the night, mind you—and, yes, it was a little like *The Big Chill*). The result is the boy Ishmael, Abraham's son by Hagar. Then, in something of a miracle, Sarah actually conceives in her old age and bears the son God has been promising all along—Isaac, the son of promise.

4. Therefore, those who come to God according to his promise of grace through Jesus—whether Jew or Gentile—are the true children of Abraham. Meanwhile, those who are still trying to earn their salvation with good behavior by keeping the law are children of slavery. And such children, Paul is convinced, "will never share in the inheritance with the free woman's son."

5. So if the law simply makes good slaves, why did God give it in the first place?

6. Answer: The law was like an adult trustee or guardian of an underage heir. Her old man has millions in a trust fund for her, available when she turns 21. In the meantime, while she's still listening to boy bands and using too much eyeliner, a guardian will mind her financial affairs for her—heaven knows she's make a mess of them, as any 14-year-old would. When this girl comes of age, however—assuming the guardian has taught her as well as he's managed her fortune—she can inherit the entire wad to do with as she pleases.

7. Likewise, before Jesus came, the law was a trustee or guardian who made people toe the line, who set curfews,

who laid down the law to keep unruly adolescents in line and prepare them for adulthood. The coming of Jesus meant the end of spiritual puberty—the law did its work, and it can retire now, thank you. For now as adults they inherit boatloads, skyfuls of grace. More wealth than they'll ever know what to do with. And it was given, unconditionally, according to promise, not earned according to law.

And there, of course, are the two metaphors with which Paul persuaded the Galatians that they didn't need to be good Jews to be good Christians: the Abraham-Hagar-Sarah story, and the underaged-heir analogy.

Opener [reflective option]

Who am I made of?

stuff you'll need

- a copy of **Who Am I Made Of?** (page 64) for each student
- pencils

Have students complete their own copies of **Who Am I Made Of?** (page 64). Then debrief the exercise by saying something like this—

Everyone resembles his or her biological parents to some degree, thanks to heredity. Even children raised by parents they're not biologically related to unconsciously exhibit habits, gestures, mannerisms, and behaviors from their biological parents.

The same is true in the spiritual realm. When we are born into God's family through faith in Christ, we pick up a family resemblance—and receive a spiritual inheritance.

Opener [artsy option]

MoMA presents...your identity in Christ

stuff you'll need

- a copy of **Who Am I in Christ?** idea sheet (page 65) for each student
- magazines to cut out pictures
- Bibles
- scissors, glue, Scotch tape, colored pencils, marking pens
- construction paper (large sheets)
- any small objects that can be added to three-dimensional art and light enough to be held with glue or tape—raid your kitchen junk drawer, and you'll have just the things

Okay, if you choose this opener, we assume your kids can get into the idea of converting the youth room into a working studio at NYC's Museum of Modern Art (MoMA). Plus, we assume your students have a substantial history of Bible lessons—read them, have been in Sunday school since they were born, and could now teach flannelgraph lessons without notes to the New Members Class. For this activity they'll be drawing on knowledge they've acquired over the years to create an abstract multimedia piece that represents a Christian's identity in Christ—art that symbolizes how a Christian is like Christ, thanks to the new birth.

You can either give each group a copy of **Who Am I in Christ?** (page 65), or you can write some of the references on a whiteboard for those students who need more ideas. To introduce the activity, say something like—

We compare photographs of a parent and child and notice similarities. Or we watch them in person, observing traits they have in common—eyes that look alike, or the chin, or the body type. Or we catch mannerisms, rhythms of speech or movement, and ways of being and doing that are the same.

It's no different for those who are, by the new birth, children of God. Our brother Jesus showed perfectly that he matched our Father God. At one time he said, "If you have seen me, you have seen the Father." We would expect to discover about ourselves, as we grow up in Christ, evidence of our inheritance—not only what we have in Christ, but what our life looks like because the same Holy Spirit who lived in Christ has moved into us, too.

In your small groups, use the media on the tables to create an abstract, symbolic piece of art that pictures for you those qualities and actions and words that make a believer look like Jesus to others.

In the Book [interview option]

S.W.W.F. fans debrief the match

stuff you'll need
- three copies of **S.W.W.F. Fans Debrief the Match** script (pages 66-67)
- an interviewer—you, or any adult or student leader—and two students as the pair of opposing fans

After performing the script on pages 66-67, ask everyone to form small groups. Write on a whiteboard the three investigations you'll ask them to make so they can focus their discussion—

- **Who were Abraham's sons, really?**
- **What did these sons symbolize for believers in Christ?**
- **What does the Jewish law itself say that the true heirs of God ought to do about the requirements of the law?**

Then say something like this—

Like an persuasive attorney, Paul appeals to the Galatian legalists on the basis of their own source material—the Mosaic law, in particular the Genesis story of Abraham and his two wives and their sons. (The Jews, remember, consider the first five books of the Bible "The Law.")

[Read Galatians 4:21-31 aloud, with as much systematic-presentation-of-evidence and courtroom flair as you can muster.]

Now, in your small groups, explore the questions on the whiteboard.

In the Book
[small group Bible-snooping option]

Woohoo! We're rich in Christ!

stuff you'll need
- a copy of **Woohoo! We're Rich in Christ!** (page 68) for each student
- Bibles
- pencils

In your small groups you'll read Paul's explanation of why we will inherit the promises God gave to Abraham. When we return from investigating the passage, we'll explore three questions:

- **Who were Abraham's sons, really?**
- **What did these sons symbolize for believers in Christ?**
- **What does the Jewish law itself say that the true heirs of God ought to do about the requirements of the law?**

You may want to write these three questions on a whiteboard to guide **Woohoo! We're Rich in Christ!** (page 68).

Closing

Eternal will & testament

stuff you'll need
- a copy of **Eternal Will & Testament** (page 69) for each student
- pencils

Hand out copies of **Eternal Will & Testament** (page 69) for everyone. Say something like—

A last will and testament, as you probably know, lists the inheritance one leaves upon death. Of course, Jesus is alive because of resurrection from the dead—but we still get his inheritance because of his death on the cross (in our place, mind you) and his resurrection. But since he's no longer dead—and, in fact, will live forever—we can't call this one a "*last* will and testament." So why not an *eternal* will and testament?

And here is what we inherit from Jesus: we are adopted into the family of God—made children of God, in fact, brothers of Jesus, and heirs or recipients of everything Christ receives from God.

There's plenty of space on the Eternal Will & Testament **you're holding for you to write how this inheritance will change your life. Think about specific areas of your life this will affect, such as parents, siblings, school, friendships, dating relationships, work, the Internet. Then briefly describe how you might be motivated to change in these areas because of your inheritance.**

Who am I made of?

First, fill in some details about you—

- ☐ Eye color ______
- ☐ Hair color ______
- ☐ Height ______
- ☐ Skin type (light, dark, brown, olive, mocha, white, black, pasty, freckled, etc.) ______
- ☐ Athletic? ______
- ☐ Generally get good grades? ______
- ☐ Kind of artsy-craftsy? Or outright artistic? ______
- ☐ Good at fixing mechanical things? ______
- ☐ Get mad or lose your temper easily? ______
- ☐ Soft-spoken or loud? ______
- ☐ Shy or outgoing? ______
- ☐ Messy or neat? ______
- ☐ Organized, or do you procrastinate a lot? ______
- ☐ Get embarrassed easily? ______
- ☐ Prefer things scheduled or spontaneous? ______
- ☐ What gestures or mannerisms of either of your parents do you think you have (tapping your fingers, playing with your hair, et cetera)?
- ☐ Do you sometimes hear yourself using any of the same phrases as either of your parents do? What are they?

Now go back and check those characteristics that you share with a parent (biological or adopted) or other adult you've grown up with or spent a lot of time with.

Now count how many items you checked...and circle that number below:

0 1 2 3 4 5 6 7 8 9 10 11 12 13 14 15 16 17

I am nothing like my parents — I am somewhat like my parents — My parents and I are twins (gag!)

IDEA SHEET

Who am I in Christ?

Member of the body of Christ
1 Corinthians 12:27

Gifted by grace
Romans 12:6

Gifted by the Spirit
Galatians 5:22-23

Alive and forgiven
Colossians 2:13

Child of God
Romans 8:15-16
Galatians 3:26

Chosen
Ephesians 1:11

Led by the Spirit
John 16:13

A new creation
2 Corinthians 5:17

Freed from sin
Romans 6:6-7

Born of the Spirit
John 3:6, 8
Galatians 4:6

An heir of God's promises
1 Peter 1:3-4
Galatians 4:28

A person of hope
1 Peter 1:3

Participator in the divine nature
2 Peter 1:4

One who delights in God's word
Romans 7:22

Not alone
John 14:18

A letter from Christ to the world
2 Corinthians 3:3

A channel of the Holy Spirit
John 7:38-39

Eternally safe
Titus 3:4-5

IDEA SHEET

Who am I in Christ?

Member of the body of Christ
1 Corinthians 12:27

Gifted by grace
Romans 12:6

Gifted by the Spirit
Galatians 5:22-23

Alive and forgiven
Colossians 2:13

Child of God
Romans 8:15-16
Galatians 3:26

Chosen
Ephesians 1:11

Led by the Spirit
John 16:13

A new creation
2 Corinthians 5:17

Freed from sin
Romans 6:6-7

Born of the Spirit
John 3:6, 8
Galatians 4:6

An heir of God's promises
1 Peter 1:3-4
Galatians 4:28

A person of hope
1 Peter 1:3

Participator in the divine nature
2 Peter 1:4

One who delights in God's word
Romans 7:22

Not alone
John 14:18

A letter from Christ to the world
2 Corinthians 3:3

A channel of the Holy Spirit
John 7:38-39

Eternally safe
Titus 3:4-5

Cast

- Interviewer (adult or student leader)
- Moses the Slasher fan (a Jewish Christian)
- Abraham Road Dog fan (a Gentile Christian)

Interviewer: With us tonight, fresh from the arena where Abraham Road Dog and Moses the Slasher were facing off, are two fans. But they seem a little deflated...like the fight wasn't all it was hyped to be. What happened?

Slasher fan: There *was* no fight. Only the fans actually fought!

Interviewer: You mean Road Dog and the Slasher were a no-show?

Road Dog fan: Oh no. They were in the ring, all right. But they started talking about there being no division between them.

Slasher fan: They'd been hoodwinked by that referee. He'll never make it in this business. He had it up on the digitizer over the ring: "In Christ's family there can be no division into Jew and non-Jew." I mean, who's going to bother with S.W.W.F. if there's no action?

Interviewer: But I mean the wrestlers—Road Dog and the Slasher—didn't they just crawl over the top of Big Boss Man to tear each other's throats out? They were rabid when we saw them before the match.

Road Dog fan: It was pure hype scripted by the marketing moguls who stood to gain from pitting the two against each other. You see, Road Dog was the first Slasher. He was the first one to be circumcised. God had made circumcision a sign of God's promise to Abraham that right-standing with God would be possible for every person—not just Jews—and it would be possible through believing God, no strings attached.

Slasher fan: So when God set himself to work on preparing the way for a savior who could make good on God's promises—who could make everlasting life with God possible, he had to set boundaries for the generations of people who would live and die before that savior came. Otherwise, there'd have been no Jewish parents for Jesus to have been born to. The whole nation would have gotten lost in the slosh of tribal wars and religions that had no clue that there is one true and living God.

Interviewer: And that's what the law was all about—what we read in Big Boss Man Paul's letter. It was to keep separate a nation of people through whom Jesus, the savior, could be born.

Road Dog fan: The three of them stood there and talked to the crowd. Told us a story about inheritances—which, yeah, we all understood. When you're a minor, it doesn't matter how rich your daddy is, you're still "handled" by teachers and trustees. You don't get to take charge of your cash until you're 21, or something.

Slasher fan: They said Abraham's promised inheritance for us was handled in the same way. The law that Moses brought from God was like the teachers and trustees who made sure the heirs could legally have full freedom to enjoy their inheritance.

Interviewer: So it turns out that everyone who believes in Jesus Christ is actually an heir of Abraham—Jews and non-Jews alike? And the law was like simple instructions for minors—meaning those who lived and died before Jesus came. Its rules were to last only until Jesus set us all free by being born under the conditions of the law and fulfilling every condition of the law.

Road Dog fan: Yeah. And all I came for was to see Road Dog flay the Slasher.

Slasher fan: Not a chance. Road Dog's a French poodle.

(*The two fans leave arguing about who would have won and how they want their money back for the tickets they bought.)*

Interviewer: Looks like it really made an impression. Let's form small groups and read through the part of Paul's letter that explains in detail what the fans heard from him in the arena.

Woohoo! We're rich in Christ!

First, talk about this—
What things do you hope to inherit from your parent(s)?

Now choose one of the following two Bible passages to read. After you read the verses, talk about the questions or statements that follow. You may want to jot down some insights your group comes up with or something memorable that one of you says.

Galatians 3:26-4:7

- Why does Paul write, "There is neither Jew nor Greek, slave nor free, male nor female..."? What does he mean?
- How are all believers related to Abraham?
- How is an heir to an estate still like a slave?
- What status and rights do we have after we place our faith in Christ? Why do we receive them?

Galatians 4:21-31

- What was the difference between Abraham's two sons?
- Who does Hagar represent? What is the significance of Mount Sinai? Why are Hagar and her children in slavery? What kind of slavery is Paul talking about?
- Who does Sarah represent? What is the "Jerusalem that is above" (verse 26)? Why is she free? How is she our mother?
- How were the Galatians like Isaac, according to Paul? How can we be like Isaac?
- What inheritance do we gain because we are "children of the promise" (verse 28)?

Eternal will & testament

I, Jesus, being of sound mind and body, declare this is my will. By my death and through my resurrection, I give to all those who receive me and believe in my name the right to become children of God (John 1:12). As such, all such heirs will become:

[List ways this inheritance will affect the different aspects of your life—parents, siblings, school, friendships, who you go out with, your job, the Internet, your future. Include how you could change in some of these aspects because of your inheritance.]

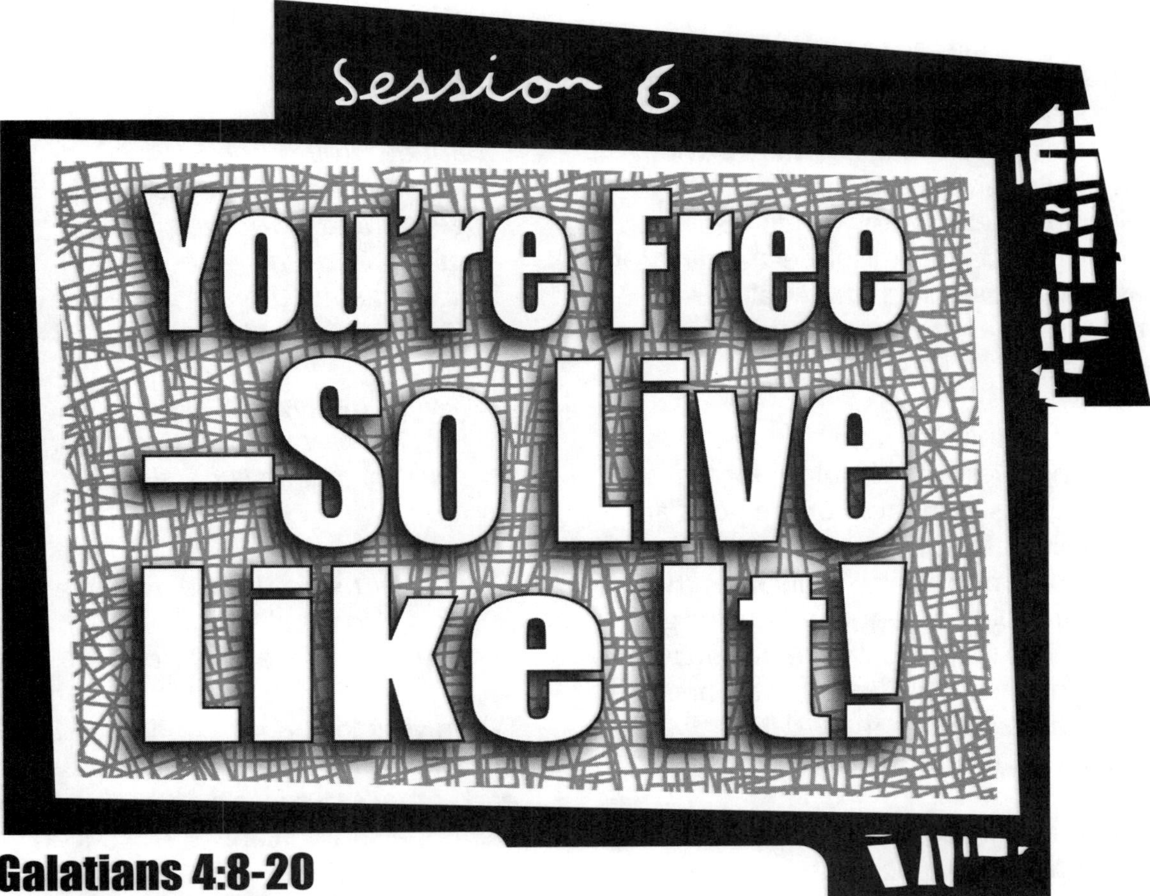

Session 6
You're Free
–So Live
Like It!

Galatians 4:8-20
Galatians 5:13-6:10

During this session students will—

- Recognize the two broad categories of fruit: fruit of the flesh and fruit of the Spirit.
- Feel that the fruit of the Spirit is worth far more to bear that the fruit of the flesh.

Inform your teaching

There are principles, and then there are principles

Despite what is commonly held by some American Christians, "a principled life" is not necessarily a desirable thing if those principles are *rules* that constrict you and distract you and enslave you. In fact, look what the apostle wrote: the Galatians were enslaved *before* they knew God (4:8), and they were apparently slipping back into the same slavery *as Christians* (4:9). Furthermore, they weren't slip-sliding into spiritual slavery via loose, boozing, womanizing paganism, but by tight, must-keep-the-rules, suffocating paganism ("weak and miserable principles...observing special days and months and seasons and years," 4:9-10).

Classic lists of Christian behavior

The classic Christian list in the Galatian letter of "the fruit of the Spirit" is only one catalog of Christian virtues that appear in Paul's letters. Skim some other of his lists so you get a well-rounded picture of Paul's idea of ideal Christian behavior:

Romans 12:9-21
1 Corinthians 13:4-8
Ephesians 5:15-6:18
Colossians 3:1-4:6
I Thessalonians 5:12-22
The entire first letter to Timothy is one big to-do list to that young pastor.
Hebrews 13:1-5

This can come as something of a surprise to Christians who are used to equating "principles" and "conservative" with godly, biblical living and "freedom from rules" and "liberal" with worldliness.

Paul corrects this misunderstanding for us as well as for first-century Galatian Christians. Paganism has always had two faces:

- A suffocating attention to rules, always looking over your shoulder for fear that priests or pastors or the gods are frowning at your shortcomings, trying to conform to narrow principles that you are told are requirements for godliness but that actually are no measure of godliness at all. (Paul invests nearly the entire letter to the Galatians with warnings against this kind of paganism.)
- An abandonment and rationalization of Christ's only rule—the law of love—a throwing off of healthy restraints, a crossing of those few boundaries that God has laid down for his children. (Almost the only place in the letter Paul warns the Galatian Christians against this kind of paganism is 5:13-24.)

In short, Paul's point in his Galatian letter is "You're free! You're free! You're free! Don't let anyone enslave you, not after Christ himself set you free! [That's 90 percent of the letter.] And by the way, don't use your freedom as an excuse to indulge your appetites." (That's 10 percent of the letter.)

Et cetera

- The Galatian letter contains some classic phrases that have found their way into everyday English as well as into Western literature (cited here in the good ol' King James Version, which is the form of most Bible passages that have worked their way into mainstream culture):

  But the fruit of the Spirit is love, joy, peace, longsuffering, gentleness, goodness, faith, meekness, temperance: against such there is no law. (5:22)

  Be not deceived; God is not mocked: for whatsoever a man soweth, that shall he also reap. (6:7)

  And let us not be weary in well doing: for in due season we shall reap, if we faint not. (6:9)

- When your kids notice it, don't let the apparent contradiction in 6:2 ("Carry each other's burdens") and 6:5 ("...for each one should carry his own load") undo them. These verses are frequently quoted in lists of biblical contradictions as evidence of the Bible's unreliability. Just look at the immediate context of each: self-sacrifice and self-evaluation, respectively. Two very different topics that happen to sit close to each other, thanks to Paul's rapid-fire salvo of closing mandates.

- Does Paul sound like his own Jewish mother here, or what?—"How I wish I could be with you now and change my tone, because I am perplexed about you!... I fear for you , that somehow I have wasted my efforts on you" (4:20,11). You can almost hear him say, "And you never call me, either..."

- "It was because of an illness that I first preached the gospel to you" (4:13)—if *that* doesn't open up some conjectures. Did a Galatian Christian take in a sick Paul, and from that incident come conversations, conversions, and finally a church?

Opener [game option]

Speed Pictionary

stuff you'll need
- Pictionary stations, one for each team. Tape large sheets of blank drawing paper on easels or walls.
- pencil or marker for each team

Don't let on that the lesson today is the fruit of the Spirit. Form teams of six and give each team pencils and a pad of paper and something hard to draw on. Tell them—

When I say *Go!* one person from every team runs to me. I'll whisper a word that you must illustrate for your team when you return to it. You may only draw, not speak or gesture or write letters. As soon as one drawer's team has guessed the word, a different team member will run to me and say to me "Word two." I'll tell her another word, and she'll illustrate *that* word for her team. And so on, for 6 words.

Since each team will have the same six words, teams must make their guesses very quietly so they don't give the answers away.

The words, if you haven't guessed by now, are three of the fruits of the Spirit and three of the fruits of the flesh as listed in Galations 5:19-21 (*idolatry, rage,* and *drunkenness*) and Galatians 5:22-23 (*love, peace*, and *self-control*).

Opener [skit option]

The orchard

stuff you'll need
- three copies of **The Orchard** script (pages 76-77)
- three impromptu student actors
- loose-fitting, long-sleeved green coat or shirt
- fake or real ivy or small boughs and leafy twigs
- one tree fruit, fake or real (apple, orange, whatever)
- flowered hat
- yellow shirt
- sunglasses

Get three volunteers to perform the skit on pages 76-77. If you have time, let them run through it once or twice before the meeting.

Debrief the skit by saying something like—

A lot of times we try to bear the fruit of the Spirit in our own strength, only to find ourselves back at square one, trying to earn God's approval again. We can be free *and* righteous—through the power of God, not our own strength.

In the Book [simulation option]

Campaigning for the Holy Spirit

stuff you'll need
- copies of all five sheets in the **Campaigning for the Holy Spirit** (pages 78-82) series
- pencils, colored pencils, crayons
- drawing paper

Unleash your kids into five groups, and ask each group to create an ad campaign for the fruit of the Holy Spirit. Each group will work with one of the following elements—
- logo
- slogan
- garment design, like front-and-back T-shirt design, shoes, or caps
- promotional giveaway novelty, for distribution through a fast-food chain
- celebrity endorsement

Introduce the ad campaign with words to this effect—

An immense amount of media communication today is advertising. A toy isn't merely a toy anymore, but a character from a soon-to-be-released Disney movie. People don't buy just novels, they buy books based on the blockbuster

movie. A T-shirt carries its manufacturer's brand.

What if we had to create a marketing portfolio that promoted the fruits of the Spirit (as opposed to living by the flesh)?

Welcome to an elite marketing agency that has just acquired a new client—that would be the Holy Spirit—to develop an ad campaign that will promote the fruits of the Spirit and cause your peers (the target audience of this ad campaign) to buy into the lifestyle characterized by the fruit of the Spirit. In different teams, you will create different aspects of this campaign.

Then distribute copies of each ad-campaign sheet on pages 78-82 to the appropriate groups. Give yourself five or ten minutes at the end of the activity for the small groups to showcase what they created. If you want, post the results of the advertising campaign around the room. If there's some really good stuff, ask the church office to insert it in next Sunday's order of worship, program, or bulletin.

In the Book
[small group Bible-snooping option]

We've got spirit (yes, we do!)

stuff you'll need
- a copy of **We've Got Spirit (Yes, We Do!)** (page 83) for each student
- Bibles
- pencils

Form small groups to read Galatians 4:8-20 and 5:13-6:10, and explain in words like this—

To circumcise or not to circumcise, and other tidbits from Moses' law...these just aren't pressing concerns of most adolescents these days. But this session's Bible passages come close to home for all Christians, not just teenagers—the trick of finding a balance between the freedom of grace and the guidance of the law. Although we can't *earn* God's love, God nevertheless helps us get better at behaving in better ways. Yes, it's a paradox—and Christianity is full of them. We are sinful *and* accepted. We are forgiven *and* need correction. We are old enough to be heirs *and* we still benefit from guardians and tutors.

Paul managed the paradox when he told the Galatians that, yes, they are free from slavery to sin and to the law, *and yet* they are still slaves—but now slaves to Christ (Romans 6:18). That means that while we can never earn God's love, we must choose to become slaves of God. Either we are slaves to sin and are judged by the law or we are slaves to Christ and are forgiven by Christ who has already paid our debt under the law.

So, in the words of ancient Israeli general Joshua, "choose for yourselves this day whom you will serve" (Joshua 24:15).

Then move on to small groups and the **We've Got Spirit (Yes, We Do!)** (page 83) handouts.

Closing

You can tell a tree by its fruit

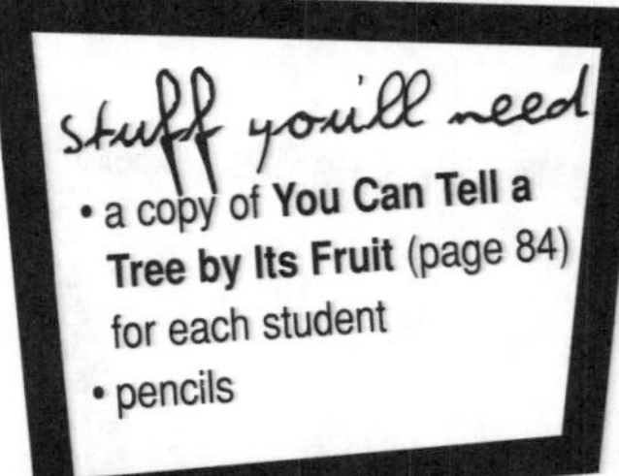

stuff you'll need
• a copy of You Can Tell a Tree by Its Fruit (page 84) for each student
• pencils

Self-evaluations are a wonderful thing. Sure, everyone needs outside input—from friends and coworkers, though sometimes you start feeling defensive in the face of criticism. But when the Holy Spirit reveals your condition directly to you, he also gives you what you need to move ahead and make progress.

Hand out copies of **You Can Tell a Tree by Its Fruit** (page 84) and encourage students to use the closing reflection time to listen to the Spirit talk to them about themselves. They can use the reproducible page to record the insights they gain.

THE ORCHARD

Cast
- Flower
- Sun
- Tree
- Birds (audience members—or play a "sounds of nature" CD in background)

Props
- flowered hat (for Flower)
- yellow shirt (for Sun)
- sunglasses (for Sun)
- loose-fitting, long-sleeved green coat or shirt (for Tree)
- fake or real ivy or small boughs and leafy twigs (for Tree)
- one tree fruit, fake or real (apple, orange, whatever)

*(**SUN** leans lazily against a wall. **FLOWER** sits cross-legged on the ground. **TREE** stands with his arms bent like branches. **BIRDS** chirp.)*

FLOWER: *(stretching and smiling)* Mmmm... Nice spring day, huh? Feels good after all that snow. Rose always says *(mockingly)*, "It's good for you, make sure you drink it all up, yadda, yadda, yadda." Me, I like the sunshine a lot better.

SUN: *(smugly)* Thanks, Flower. Just trying to do my job. *(settles back in against the wall)*

TREE: *(starts groaning and grunting with eyes tightly shut)* NNNGGHHH.... uuuhhhnngg...grrrrrr... *(**FLOWER** looks curiously at **TREE**, and **SUN** tips his shades down his nose to get a better look at **TREE**, who continues moaning occasionally and tensing his branches.)*

SUN: What's up with him? Do you think I made him sick? I've been turning it up pretty strong, lately, y'know, what with summer coming and all.

FLOWER: I don't know what's wrong with him. Hey, Tree! *(**TREE** continues to grunt and groan.)*...I said, TREE!

TREE: *(stops groaning, opens one eye at **FLOWER**, and snaps at her)* So whaddaya want?

FLOWER: *(innocently)* What're you doing?

TREE: Can't you *see* what I'm doing? I'm busy now! Can't you just go away and leave me alone?

FLOWER: *(sarcastically)* Oh, sure, a tree that grunts and groans, I know exactly what you're doing—NO, of COURSE I don't know what you're doing. And no, I *can't* go away because, if you didn't notice, I have *roots* and having *roots* means you don't really go anywhere.

SUN: I think she's busting your branches, buddy.

TREE: Awright already. Since you've already interrupted me, I may as well enlighten you both.

*(***FLOWER** *and* **SUN** *roll their eyes at each other.)*

TREE: I think it should be obvious that I am hard at work. *(Pompously)* I'm bearing fruit. Now, since it's very strenuous work, if you'll excuse me, I'm very busy.

*(***FLOWER** *and* **SUN** *pause for a minute, then look at each other and break into gales of laughter.)*

TREE: *(taken aback)* What? *(***SUN** *and* **FLOWER** *continue laughing.)* WHAT?

FLOWER: *(wiping away tears of mirth)* Don't you know—oh, this is killin' me—you don't have to *try* to bear fruit—it just happens? Trees just bear fruit! *(Starts laughing again.)*

TREE: *(suspiciously)* What do you mean they *just* bear fruit? It takes a lot of hard work! Can't you see? It doesn't "just happen"! I have to do my branch exercises *(moves branches as if pumping iron)*, take my fruit vitamins, shake my leaves to chase away all the bugs and birds *(motions with his hands)*, and squeeze REALLY hard. If I work hard enough, then POP! POP! POP! *(***FLOWER** *and* **SUN** *jump at each "POP!")* I've done it! I'll have some excellent, shiny, juicy fruit hanging from these strong branches of mine *(flexes)* and everyone will come to me, saying what great fruit I've got, what a great job I did. Believe me, I'm ALL THAT...and pesticide-free, too.

SUN: That is the most ridiculous thing I've ever heard.

FLOWER: Tree, don't you know? Bearing fruit isn't about work. I mean, yes, the Good Gardener once said "you'll know a tree by its fruit," but he didn't mean trees have to *exercise* to bear fruit! If a tree gets lots of water and sun, then fruit really *does* just grow! I mean, c'mon—you're a fruit tree. Bearing fruit is what you were made to do. Fruit happens!

SUN: She's right, man. GG himself makes us grow. I can shine down all you want, and the clouds can rain down all you want, but only that Big Gardener in the Sky can make fruit POP. Trying to make that fruit happen yourself, well, it simply isn't what makes fruit appear.

(Suddenly, **TREE** *makes popping noises and "produces" fruit, from his sleeves, into his hands.)*

TREE: *(surprised)* Look at that now, would ya! You're right—I wasn't even trying!

SUN *and* **FLOWER:** *(nod and smile together)* You shoot that fruit, now, 'kay?

END

Campaigning for the Holy Spirit

Ad Agency:	**Your Group**
Client:	**Holy Spirit**
Job:	**Promotion of client's fruits**

Logo

You work for an advertising agency. You've just signed up the Holy Spirit as a client, and he wants some positive promotion and accurate publicity for the fruits available to believers in Jesus—you know, love, joy, peace, patience, kindness, goodness, faithfulness, gentleness, the works (Galatians 5:22-23).

Your team's task is to design a logo for your client—a simple yet distinct image or icon that symbolizes or represents the nature and function of these fruits of the Holy Spirit. For starters, think of widely recognized corporate logos—the golden-arched M of McDonalds, the blue-lined ball of AT&T, Nike's swoosh. They're simple, and they symbolize the essence of the client.

So whip out some drawing paper and put those colored pencils or crayons to work—you're on deadline! This is an important client you don't want to lose.

After you've developed a logo you're satisfied with, be prepared to explain it to the other teams in your agency—which, by the way, are working on other aspects of this ad campaign.

Campaigning for the Holy Spirit

Ad Agency:	**Your Group**
Client:	**Holy Spirit**
Job:	**Promotion of client's fruits**

Slogan

You work for an advertising agency. You've just signed up the Holy Spirit as a client, and he wants some positive promotion and accurate publicity for the fruits available to believers in Jesus—you know, love, joy, peace, patience, kindness, goodness, faithfulness, gentleness, the works (Galatians 5:22-23).

Your team's task is to write a slogan for your client—a simple, brief, clever-but-not-cutesy statement that summarizes, reflects, or represents the nature and function of these fruits of the Holy Spirit. For starters, think of widely recognized slogans—the now-outdated "Just do it" of Nike...Microsoft's "So where do you want to go today?"...your local TV news station's slogan, which is "All the news, all the time," or something close to that. Slogans are simple and suggest a feeling the client wants to create in the listener or reader.

So whip out your laptops and yellow pads—okay, blank unlined paper will do, because you're on deadline! After all, this is an important client you don't want to lose.

After you've fine-tuned a slogan you're satisfied with, be prepared to explain it to the other teams in your agency—which, by the way, are working on other aspects of this ad campaign.

Campaigning for the Holy Spirit

Ad Agency:	**Your Group**
Client:	**Holy Spirit**
Job:	**Promotion of client's fruits**

Garment Design

You work for an advertising agency. You've just signed up the Holy Spirit as a client, and he wants some positive promotion and accurate publicity for the fruits available to believers in Jesus—you know, love, joy, peace, patience, kindness, goodness, faithfulness, gentleness, the works (Galatians 5:22-23).

Your team's task is to create garment designs that reflect and promote your client's fruits—a front-and-back T-shirt design, say, or shoes, caps, etc. You know what your friends wear—in fact, your friends are the client's target audience—so create a design that can go on a shirt or jacket or cap or footwear that reflects the nature and function of these fruits of the Holy Spirit. Colors are important, size of images or words you may want to use on the garment are also important, as is placement of the images of words—on the sleeve? on front center, or on a pocket? Or do you even want pockets?. Remember that whatever you design should be simple and should suggest the essence of the client.

So whip out some drawing paper and put those colored pencils or crayons to work—you're on deadline! After all, this is an important client you don't want to lose.

Show more than one perspective—like front and back of a shirt, both sides and maybe the tread of a shoe, etc. Be prepared to explain it to the other teams in your agency—which, by the way, are working on other aspects of this ad campaign.

Campaigning for the Holy Spirit

Ad Agency:	**Your Group**
Client:	**Holy Spirit**
Job:	**Promotion of client's fruits**

Promotional giveaway novelty/fast-food distribution

You work for an advertising agency. You've just signed up the Holy Spirit as a client, and he wants some positive promotion and accurate publicity for the fruits available to believers in Jesus—you know, love, joy, peace, patience, kindness, goodness, faithfulness, gentleness, the works (Galatians 5:22-23).

Your team's task is to create a promotional, giveaway novelty or knick-knack for your client that you will distribute through a fast-food chain to adolescent customers, who are known to eat vast quantities of fast food—a clever little something that suggests or represents the nature and function of these fruits of the Holy Spirit. The novelty may be functional—perform some practical task, like a bottle opener—aesthetic, just look cool, some combination of those two traits, or be something else entirely. They may be a single item or a set of several similar but different items. And, of course, the novelty must appeal to adolescents. Which means no mini-troll dolls with purple hair.

Furthermore, you must decide *which* fast-food restaurant will distribute these novelties. Which franchise best suits your client and your client's fruits?

So whip out some paper to brainstorm and sketch on...put those colored pencils or crayons to work—you're on deadline! After all, this is an important client you don't want to lose.

After you've designed a promotional novelty (or line of novelties) you're satisfied with—and selected the right fast-food franchise to distribute your giveaway—be prepared to explain your item and your reasoning to the other teams in your agency (which, by the way, are working on other aspects of this ad campaign).

Campaigning for the Holy Spirit

Ad Agency:	**Your Group**
Client:	**Holy Spirit**
Job:	**Promotion of client's fruits**

Celebrity endorsement

You work for an advertising agency. You've just signed up the Holy Spirit as a client, and he wants some positive promotion and accurate publicity for the fruits available to believers in Jesus—you know, love, joy, peace, patience, kindness, goodness, the works (Galatians 5:22-23).

Your team's task is to acquire a celebrity endorsement for your client's fruits—a short statement from someone—

- Who already has something in common with the client and the fruits, so that what the celebrity says is credible (forget anyone associated with the National Hockey League or WWF)
- Who is admired by most adolescents, the target audience of this campaign

So you need to think of an appropriate celebrity, then write an endorsement that sounds like the celebrity wrote it. Of course, you'll send a draft of the endorsement to the celebrity so that he or she has a chance to agree with himself or herself.

The endorsement should be brief, personal, warm, believable, and should emphasize something about what the fruit of the Holy Spirit specifically means to him or her.

So whip out your laptops and yellow pads—okay, blank unlined paper will do just as well—because you're on deadline! This is an important client you don't want to lose.

After you've selected a celebrity and fine-tuned an endorsement, be prepared to explain your reasoning to the other teams in your agency—which, by the way, are working on other aspects of this ad campaign.

We've got spirit (yes, we do!)

First, talk about this—
Do you have trouble following rules? Why or why not?

Now choose one of the following four Bible passages to read. After reading the verses, talk about the questions or statements that follow. You may want to jot down some insights your group comes up with, or something memorable that one of you may say.

Galatians 4:8-20

- What in Paul's words clue you in to how he feels about his Galatians readers? Why is he writing to them?
- What kind of slavery are the Galatians returning to?
- How does Paul describe the motives of the false teachers?

Galatians 5:13-18

- Paul told the Galatians they were free from the law—so how does he urge them to use their freedom? Why?
- What does Paul imply the Galatians want to do in verse 17? What keeps them from doing it?
- Paul appeals to the law in verse 14. Why is this particularly appropriate in a letter to the Galatians of all people?

Galatians 5:18-26

- What similarities and differences are there between Paul's list of the *acts of the sinful nature* and the *fruit of the Spirit*?
- Briefly describe the lifestyle of someone you know who demonstrates one spiritual fruit very well.
- What do you think Paul means, one minute writing that salvation is a gift that we **can't** earn by good behavior, and the next minute writing, "Those who live like this will not inherit the kingdom of God" (verse 21)?
- What does it mean to crucify our sinful nature?

Galatians 6:1-10

- What does it mean to reap what you sow?
- How do people sow to please the sinful nature—and what are the results? How do people sow to please the Spirit, and what are the results?
- Why do you think it is so stinking hard to respect the boundaries God sets for our lives?
- By the way, just what *are* some of those boundaries?

Finally...

- Anything in these verses that's a puzzle to you? That just doesn't make sense?
- What one thing got your attention most of all in these verses? Why did it affect you like it did?

You can tell a tree by its fruit

Fruit has different stages of development. Fruit is a bud before it becomes a flower. Then the flower drops off and a bulge of new, very green fruit shows. In time you can actually recognize what fruit it's going to be, even though it's not ready to pick. And finally the mature fruit ripens, and the one who picks it enjoys a sweet treat.

Get the picture? Mark on the lines below to indicate where you think you are with each of the spiritual fruits.

love

wrong tree | still in the bud | the flower is set | small green fruit | ripe and ready to pick!

joy

wrong tree | still in the bud | the flower is set | small green fruit | ripe and ready to pick!

peace

wrong tree | still in the bud | the flower is set | small green fruit | ripe and ready to pick!

patience

wrong tree | still in the bud | the flower is set | small green fruit | ripe and ready to pick!

kindness

wrong tree | still in the bud | the flower is set | small green fruit | ripe and ready to pick!

goodness

wrong tree | still in the bud | the flower is set | small green fruit | ripe and ready to pick!

faithfulness

wrong tree | still in the bud | the flower is set | small green fruit | ripe and ready to pick!

gentleness

wrong tree | still in the bud | the flower is set | small green fruit | ripe and ready to pick!

self-control

wrong tree | still in the bud | the flower is set | small green fruit | ripe and ready to pick!

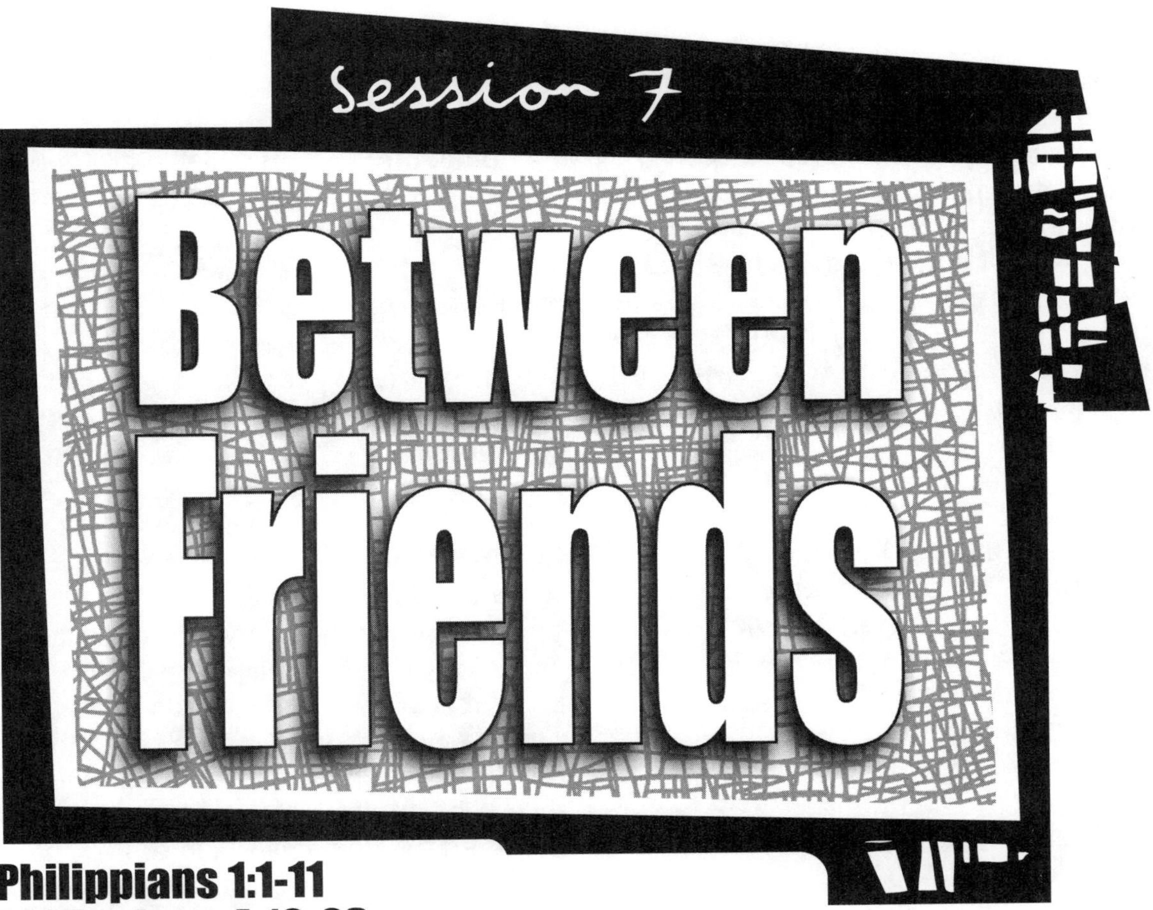

Philippians 1:1-11
Philippians 4:10-23

During this session students will—

- Identify key characteristics of good friendships.
- Feel motivated to encourage and care for their own friends by reading the story of Paul being encouraged and cared for by *his* friends.

Life is difficult

...even for a Christian—which is why everyone needs at least one close friend, a soulmate, someone you'd do almost anything for, someone who does almost anything for you.

Set yourself up to feel what Philippians is all about by connecting with a close friend. Let them know the things about their friendship that mean a lot to you.

Then think of someone whose life you have touched in the past, and reconnect with this person, too, by giving that person something or some communication that you know will support them.

Inform your teaching

Friends understand, comprehend, and appreciate

Paul's letter to the Christians in Philippi is so bone-jarring in some ways—he ends one subject and starts another with absolutely *no* warning—that some biblical scholars think the letter we call "Philippians" is actually a compilation of three letters Paul wrote to this church. The letter simply defies any linear organization. As further evidence for the multi-letter theory, these experts point to the apostle's words, "It's no trouble for me to write the same things to you *again*" (3:1, emphasis added).

Others disagree, explaining that Paul's whiplash segues are merely evidence of a very personal letter to intimate friends—the kind of letter you write when your friend recognizes immediately what you're writing about without you having to explain everything in detail. You and your friend have enough history together that just a phrase evokes entire experiences you've shared. So naturally, you can jump around a lot, ramble here and there, interrupt a train of thought with a reminiscence, then double back to where you left off again. After all, this isn't a seminary thesis. It's a letter to your *friend*, for crying out loud.

Luv u!

Philippians is that kind of letter. Whether it's a compilation or whether it arrived in a Macedonian mailbox in a single envelope, most everyone agrees that it's a particularly intimate letter. The letter is dripping with Paul's love for these people. Look at the forms it takes—

- *Intimacy*. "I have you in my heart," the apostle writes (1:7).
- *Desire*. "I long for all of you" (1:8).
- *Gratitude*. Especially this. "It was good of you to share in my troubles," Paul wrote (4:14, 16). "You sent me aid again and again when I was in need"—specifically, for what sounds like a very practical gift, especially when you remember that Paul was writing from a prison (see **Letter from Block B, Cell 27**, at right). Was it a cash gift? Extra rations of food? Winter clothing? A care package of warm socks and hot chocolate? Such practical deliveries were not unknown—Paul wrote to Timothy to "bring the cloak that I left with Carpus at Troas, and my scrolls" (2 Timothy 4:13).

The courier

Whatever it was, the gift came via Epaphroditus (ee-pafro-DYE-tus)—"my brother, fellow worker and fellow soldier, who is also your messenger, whom you sent to take care of my needs" (Philippians 2:25). Epaphroditus was undoubtedly a pagan-turned-Christian, what with a name that means *belonging to Aphrodite*, or Venus, the Greek goddess of love. After he had delivered the Philippians' gift to Paul, he had apparently stayed around and been of immense and necessary help to Paul—

It was probably the Philippian church that Paul bragged on to Christians in Corinth in 2 Corinthians 8:1-5. The Christians in Philippi—a city in the province of Macedonia—apparently gave a generous gift of cash to Paul or to a cause of Paul's, even though they lived in poverty themselves.

Letter from Block B, Cell 27

You've got to be a Pauline-epistle trivia nut to enjoy this: his letter to the Philippian Christians was clearly written from prison—but what prison? The reference to a "palace guard" (1:13) and "Caesar's household" (4:22) seem obvious allusions to a Roman imprisonment—but the book just doesn't have that late-in-life feel to Pauline scholars, like 2 Timothy. Most agree that Paul was in Rome only during the final years of his life.

During the 20th century, however, an inscription was discovered that indicated "the presence of a detachment of the Praetorian Guard as well as members of Caesar's household" in Ephesus—a discovery that puts Ephesus on the list of possible cities from which was written the letter to the Philippians. (The Wycliffe Bible Commentary, Charles F. Pfeiffer and Everett F. Harrison [eds.]Chicago: Moody Press, 1962; writer of Philippians commentary: Robert H. Mounce).*

*The Praetorian Guard was an elite squad of imperial soldiers pledged to protect the Roman emperor—kind of the Secret Service meets the Navy SEALs.

in the process becoming ill and almost dying. This letter of Philippians is something of a thank-you note—with large helpings of encouragement and warnings—Paul *is* the writer, after all!—sent back to Philippi by the hand of, again, Epaphroditus (2:25-30).

Gratitude for the gift (whatever it was), for lending Paul Epaphroditus for quite a while, for the Philippians' unwavering partnership with him—it all pointed to an intimate and cherished love between friends.

A friend in need

For all the fiascos that friends can cause for each other—especially among adolescents—no one wishes for friendlessness. The strength and support and love friends can give each other is worth the risk of getting mixed up in the wrong crowd. Besides, trying to keep teenagers from their friends, or from making friends, is like trying to keep an outdoor cat indoors—sooner or later, the door will hang open just one second too long, and out they'll shoot. Kids *will* find a way to their friends, for good or ill.

This session explores the intimate friendship between Paul and the Philippian church, and what it means for you and your students.

Opener [creative writing option]

How to be a good friend

Stuff you'll need
- A copy of **How to Be a Good Friend** (page 90) for each student
- pencils

Either in small groups or individually, prep your kids for this activity with words to this effect—

We're going to see that Paul and the Philippians had a deep and intimate friendship. What makes such a friendship, anyway? Openness? Honesty? An easy willingness to share?

Let's think for a few minutes about the kind of friends *we'd* like to be to others—which isn't a bad strategy for making friends, because people attract the kind of friends that they are themselves.

Then hand out copies of **How to Be a Good Friend** (page 90), and let the kids work through them.

Opener [interactive reading option]

The great "Everybody together now!" interactive responsive reading

Before you or one or more students read Philippians 1:1-11 and 4:10-23 aloud, prep your group this way—

- **Whenever you hear the words *I* or *me*, shout together, "WHO, *ME*?"**
- **Whenever you hear the words *you* or *your*, shout, "YES, *YOU*!"**
- **Whenever you hear a name for God (*God*, *Jesus*, *Christ*, et cetera), sing the words, "JOY TO THE WORLD!"**
- **When you hear the word *gospel*, declare, "AMEN!"**

With any luck, the Harvesters Bible study on the other side of the church building will think you're having a Pentecostal service. Whoop it up!

In the Book
[small group Bible-snooping option]

Scratch the surface of an intimate friendship, and you'll find gratitude

> stuff you'll need
> - a copy of **Just between Friends** (page 91) for each student
> - Bibles
> - pencils

To make the transition to the Bible study, choose what points from below you want to make, summarize them in your own words—or, if you prefer, just read them verbatim.

- **Paul's letter to the Christians at Philippi—technically called "The Letter of St. Paul to the Philippians"—is a very personal letter, because everything in it points to the fact that they and Paul were intimate friends. He had been visited there in Philippi at least once, spent some time with the Christians there, he knew individuals, and he could picture them as he wrote to them.**

- **And just like you do in letters or e-mail messages you write to your best friend, he jumped around a lot without explaining everything in detail. He changes subjects abruptly, interrupts a train of thought with a reminiscence, then doubles back to where he left off. So as we study this letter, don't let his spiraling around confuse you. It's just a letter to dear friends who can almost read his thoughts.**

- **This letter is especially full of *gratitude*. You'll see this as we read it. What Paul had most on his mind to be thankful for was the gift the Philippians had sent him via a messenger named Epaphroditus (ee-pafro-DYE-tus). The way Paul wrote, it seemed a very practical gift, especially considering that Paul was writing from a prison. It could have been cash, extra rations of food, winter clothing—maybe a first-century care package of warm socks and hot chocolate. In any case, Paul just couldn't get over how thoughtful and generous the Philippians had been to him.**

Then distribute **Just between Friends** (page 91) to all the students, get into small groups (preferably with an adult in each group), and let 'em start talking about the passage.

What does it mean?
[role-play option]

Friendship dilemmas

> stuff you'll need
> - Slips from **Friendship Dilemmas** (page 92)

Say something to this effect—

One reason a friendship becomes close or intimate is because you and your friend survive a tough time between you. In friendship as in the rest of life, problems can strengthen you.

If your youth group is on the small side, have different students role-play the scenarios in **Friendship Dilemmas** (page 92). If your youth group is larger, divide into small groups, give them each a slip from **Friendship Dilemmas**, and let them role-play solutions in their small groups.

Just for fun—and for contrast—have kids role-play how *not* to deal with one or two of the predicaments.

Closing

Be a giving friend this week

Tell the students words to this effect—

Paul's gratitude to the Philippians for whatever their gift to him was, his gratitude for their lending him Epaphroditus for quite a while, his gratitude for the Philippians' unwavering partnership with him—it all pointed to an intimate and cherished love between friends.

Even though friends can cause craziness for each other, no one wants to be friendless. No one ought to be friendless. Friends are strength, support, encouragement, and clarity when life gets tough. These are gifts that intimate friends give each other.

Think this week what gifts your friends need, and what gifts you can give them. Think broadly—the gift that is needed can be very concrete (like the food or clothing or whatever the Philippians sent Paul) or maybe just your silent presence during an especially hard time.

If your group is small enough, some students may respond to your invitation to share what gift that is, without mentioning the name of the friend they're thinking of.

Close with a prayer. You may want to close each of these sessions on Philippians for the next few weeks with a prayerful passage in Philippians 1:9-11 (adapted slightly for group prayer).

And this is our prayer: that our love
may abound more and more in
knowledge and depth of insight,
So that we may be able to discern
what is best and may be pure and
blameless until the day of Christ,
Filled with the fruit of righteousness
that comes through Jesus Christ—
to the glory and praise of God.
Amen.

How to be a good friend

Those who are good friends find good friends. Although we'd all like to choose the perfect friend—or perfect parent, girlfriend or boyfriend, boss, and so on—it's easier to change yourself than to change someone else.

So be intentional for a few minutes about the kind of friend you'd like to be if you could. Dream a little—just for fun, redesign yourself into the kind of friend you'd like to be.

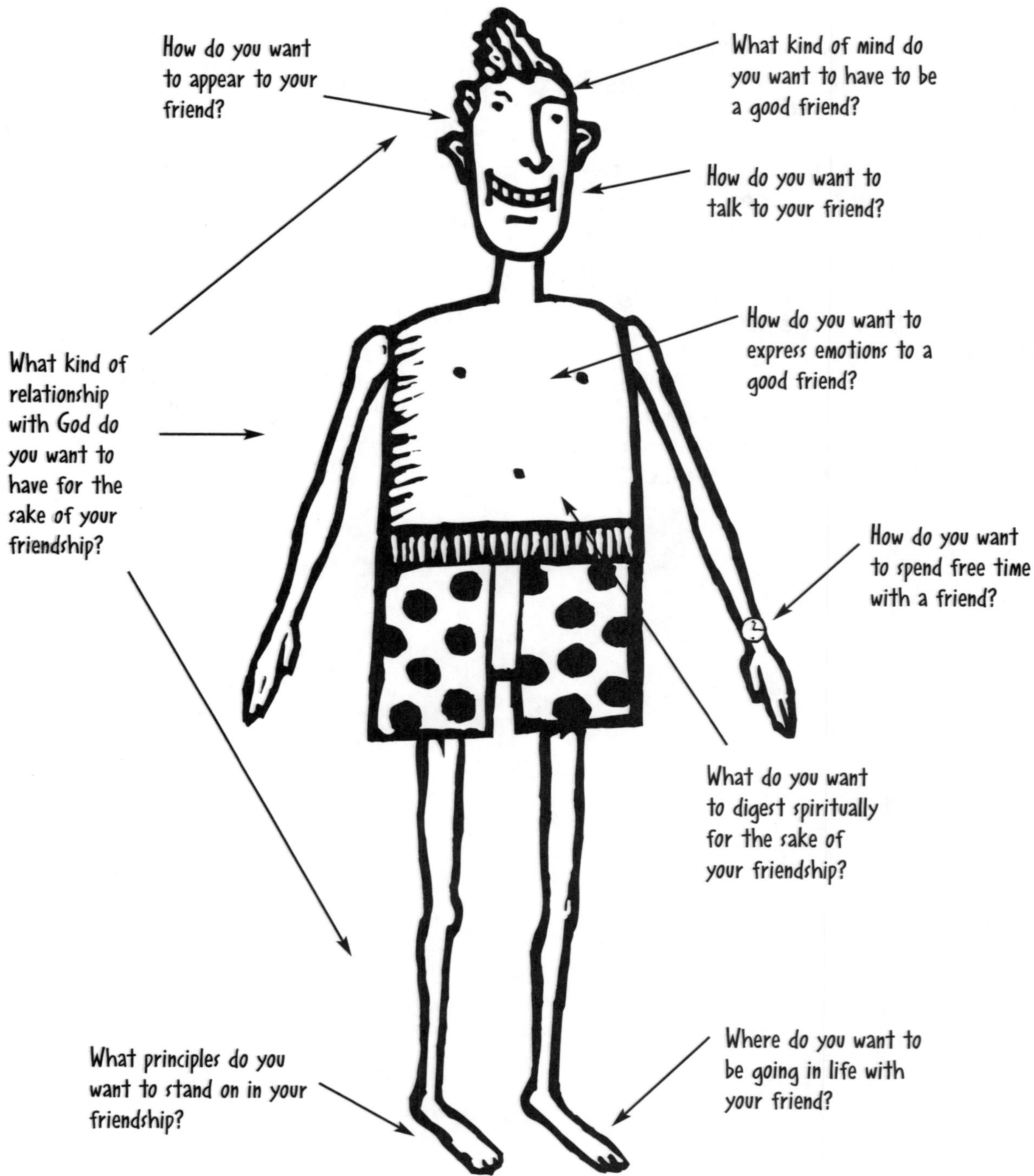
How do you want to appear to your friend?
What kind of mind do you want to have to be a good friend?
How do you want to talk to your friend?
How do you want to express emotions to a good friend?
What kind of relationship with God do you want to have for the sake of your friendship?
How do you want to spend free time with a friend?
What do you want to digest spiritually for the sake of your friendship?
What principles do you want to stand on in your friendship?
Where do you want to be going in life with your friend?

Just between friends...

First, talk about this—

- What made an intimate friend when you were very young (one who gave me her Cracker Jack prize, one who let me use his baseball mitt when he was batting, et cetera)?
- What makes an intimate friend *now* (you can actually tell an intimate friend what you dreamed last night, an intimate friend is one you can invite on a family vacation, et cetera)?
- Talk about something a friend did for you or gave you that you are really, really grateful for—something you'll never forget, something that you've measured all friendships against since then?
- Talk about what that friendship—or any intimate friendship—may have cost you—what did you miss as a result of being with your intimate friend? What little or big irritating habits did you put up with for the sake of that friendship? What about *you* did your friend have to put up with?

After reading Philippians 1:1-11 and 4:10-23, talk about three or four of these questions that appeal to your group. You may want to jot down some insights your group comes up with or something memorable that one of you may say.

- What is it about the Philippians that they rank so high in Paul's estimation? If it seems like he's bragging on them, why?
- Pick out a few details about the Philippians that Paul is particularly grateful for.
- In this friendship between Paul and the Christians at Philippi, what does Paul say he receives from them? What does Paul say they get from him?
- What does Paul want for his friends at Philippi?

Finally...

- Anything in these verses that's a puzzle to you? That just doesn't make sense?
- What one thing got your attention most of all in these verses? Why did it affect you like it did?

Friendship dilemmas

Mall run

A friend of yours offers to drive you to the mall five miles away. On the way there, you put two and two together and realize that he took his parents' car without their knowing it. And that he failed his driver's test last week.

What do you do?

Wannabe with you

You usually eat lunch with a few good friends. But someone you don't know very well has started sitting with you and trying to make conversation. It's apparent that this person doesn't really have any friends and is trying hard to fit in—too hard, in fact—and not succeeding at it. Yet you have hardly any classes with these friends this year, and lunch is the about the only time you can connect with them.

What do you do?

Love versus you

One of your close friends starts dating a new girlfriend, and it's not long before he's with her almost all the time—and he hardly hangs with you at all. What's curious is that you know they often argue, even in public, yet they never go anywhere without each other. You wonder what their relationship is like—it doesn't seem all that healthy to you—but they haven't asked you for advice. Besides, it's probably just your hurt feelings at being "dropped" as his best friend.

What do you do?

Ivy League friend

One of your friends has just been accepted to Stanford, say, or Princeton—a top-rate, exclusive school, in any case. At first she is happy about it, as anyone would be. Then you notice that whenever your group of friends talks about colleges, she always name-drops Stanford and makes sure everyone understands how elite it is. In short, your friend quickly becomes obnoxious. She's still your friend and all—but it's kind of hard, since you haven't even heard from the colleges you applied to: a couple of state colleges, one in town and one three hours away. You're just getting tired of being constantly reminded of how great she and her Ivy League school are.

What do you do?

Session 8: The Gospel Is Bigger Than Me

Philippians 1:12-26

During this session students will—

- Recognize that God's work may get done in ways that they don't understand or agree with—or even by people whose motives are plainly wrong.
- Understand that despite the loss, grief, and often tragedy in death, the death of a Christian is a welcome into the presence of Christ.

Inform your teaching

Sometimes it's just the deed that counts (and forget the motive)

You probably wouldn't want to know how many Christian churches and denominations, how many Christian organizations and agencies and businesses, were started in order to do the work of the gospel in the "right" way. Find five similar churches in a town, and because none of them does worship in quite the "right" way, another church pops up to make sure that the "right" way gets done. Find a dozen Christian organizations in the country whose goals are almost identical—caring for third-world children, or publishing Christian books, or recruiting and training missionaries—and you'll find a dozen more start up in order to do the work the "right" way.

Not that variety and diversity are bad.

It's not about you

The work of the gospel, the sharing of the love and power of Jesus, doesn't have to be done your way for it to get done. This week do a heart-level check on your own motives for ministry. What are your motives for leading or working with your youth group? Are your motives tinged just a little with wanting to keep kids from migrating to the megachurch across town that has its own youth gym, youth band, and youth service every Saturday night? Or with the conviction that you're doing youth work "right"—not wrong like the other churches in town? Or are you in youth ministry simply (though probably unconsciously) to boost your ego or to put yourself in a place where you're valued?

We need lots of ways to do what Christians need to do for the world and for each other. It just makes one wonder what an organization's motives are for launching itself. Is it thinking—

- "Finally, we're gonna do this job the right way, the biblical way, not like Ministry A or Organization B—in fact, I sometimes wonder if they're even Christian."
- "Hey, Christians are buying this stuff like crazy. Let's get in there and make some profit on it."
- "Whoa, our radio ministry competitor is pulling huge ratings. We can't be left behind...gotta increase our market share."

The good news, the Bible says, is that the gospel work is getting done, regardless of motives. At least that's what Paul wrote to the Philippians.

> *It is true that some preach Christ out of envy and rivalry, but others out of goodwill. The latter do so in love, knowing that I am put here for the defense of the gospel. The former preach Christ out of selfish ambition, not sincerely, supposing that they can stir up trouble for me while I am in chains. But what does it matter? The important thing is that in every way, whether from false motives or true, Christ is preached. And because of this I rejoice.* (1:15-18)

This is not an easy truth to swallow. That other Christians do the work of the ministry in ways you don't agree with may irritate you, offend you, may actually punish you—but if the gospel is getting to the people who need it, sometimes it just doesn't matter if you like how it's getting there. Sometimes doing a Christian task your way just gets in the way.

Paul wrote that the gospel was more important than his ego, his feelings, even his well-being. Prison, beatings, competitors' or adversaries' dubious motives for ministering—none of these mattered to Paul. Others would have to answer to God about their motives and methods, not to Paul. All Paul cared about was that the gospel was getting out there, and that's what it was all about, and that was enough.

A good death

Never far from Paul's mind was the prospect of death, basically because his message stirred up such hatred among some listeners (usually the ones who stood to lose influence and power if Paul's message were accepted by the masses). Yet to Paul death was hardly an event to be grieved. "For to me, to live is Christ," he wrote, "and to die is gain." And he had a tough time choosing which was better—living or dying.

> *If I am to go on living in the body, this will mean fruitful labor for me. Yet what shall I choose? I do not know! I am torn between the two: I desire to depart and be with Christ, which is better by far; but it is more necessary for you that I remain in the body.*

This was a huge thing for Philippian readers to grasp. The idea of heaven may be commonplace to the 21st-century industrialized and Christianized West, but what the typical Greek grew up with in ancient times was the idea of *hades*, the gray, nondescript dwelling of the dead and departed—only one destination for all the dead—of shadow-souls, cut off from the sun and color and senses and delights of this world. Not exactly a fiery hell of eternal punishment, but not anything to look forward to, either.

So to read Paul actually *anticipating* death was a new and hopeful twist on religion in the ancient world. Not that Paul had a death wish, but only that he recognized physical death not as The End, but as a transition to a better mode of existence: to be with Christ! It doesn't get any better than that, he wrote. Yet he was willing to postpone his own pleasure (!) for the sake of Christians in Philippi and elsewhere who still needed him.

This is a tenet that puts Christianity at odds with paganism, whether ancient or modern. There are worse things than the death of a believer, Christianity teaches, as grievous or horrific as that death may be. As darkest midnight must come before the dawn, as Good Friday must come before Easter Sunday, so death must be passed through before one enters the best of all times and places: eternity with the living Jesus who's been lovingly dogging your footsteps for all your earthly life, and whom now you see, finally, face to face.

Opener
[strange-but-true option]

Good news or goofy news?

stuff you'll need
- a copy of **Good News of the Gospel—or Just Goofy News?** (pages 99-101) for each student
- pencils

Take a look at **Good News of the Gospel—or Just Goofy News?** (pages 99-101) before you lead this activity, which introduces the idea of motives behind and methods of Christian evangelization or outreach. As you probably already know, Paul was fairly tolerant in this matter (see **Inform Your Teaching** at the beginning of this session)—probably more tolerant than your students.

But let's find out. You can do this activity in a number of ways, so choose the way that fits your group, its size, its sophistication, et cetera. Try it all together as one group, while you read the items aloud and students react...or together in one group with each student individually completing the sheet...or in small groups, each student with her own sheet, or a leader reading the items and facilitating discussion...or whatever works for you.

Opener
[current events investigation option]

News search—good, goofy, worst

stuff you'll need
- a stack of old newspapers, back issues of magazines—*Time, Newsweek, U.S. News & World Report, Christianity Today* (point to students to the news section in the back half), *Charisma*, some of your *Youthworker* issues (the "Update" section), et cetera
- a slip for each small group, cut apart from a photocopy of **News Search—Good, Goofy, Worst** (page 102)
- a goofy prize—like the newstand issue of *The National Enquirer* or a similar Madonna-Has-Alien's-Baby gossip sheet
- pencils

In small groups, have your kids look through the newspapers and magazines for nominees for the following categories.

- Best Good News
- Goofiest Good News
- Good News Achieved in the Worst Way
- Best Achievement by Worst Person
- Worst Achievement by Best Person

Photocopy this list of categories in **News Search–Good, Goofy, Worst** (page 102), and cut the slips apart for your small groups. Create more categories (or different categories) if you want, too. Of course, if students are particularly aware of current events or know their history, they can nominate present or past news items they know about, whether or not they're in your newspapers or magazines.

Take 10 minutes or so—and if you want, leave time at the end for small groups to share their finds with everyone.

In the Book
[small group Bible-snooping option]

Wrong motive, good deaths

stuff you'll need
- Copies of **Wrong Motives, Good Deaths** (page 103) for each student
- pencils

To make the transition to the Bible study, say something like—

As we've seen, good news comes in all kinds, varieties, and shades. And sometimes good news comes in unexpected packages.

Now choose points from below that you want to make and summarize them in your own words—or, if you prefer, just read them verbatim.

About motives...

- **You've heard people say—or said yourself, after a mediocre gift was given—or after a failed attempt at doing something good: "Well, it was the thought that counts." Here in chapter 1 of his letter to the Philippians, Paul says the opposite: It's the *deed* that counts, not the thought. Or you can say it this way: "So someone did a good thing for wrong motives? So what?"**

- **Paul isn't being flippant here, but he is pointing out what's really important when it comes to the ministry of the gospel—getting the good news out to the people who need it. Paul points out that since news got around that he was in jail, others picked up where he left off and started preaching and sharing like crazy. Some of these Christians did the work of the ministry to support Paul, while others did it to compete with him, or because they were jealous of his success and wanted the same star billing that Paul got.**

- **And how did Paul react, when all this got back to him in his damp, cold jail cell? Big deal, he said—I don't care *why* they're speaking the Word of God, whether to hurt me or help me. The gospel was more important than his ego, he wrote, bigger than his feelings, bigger than even his well-being. Prison, beatings, competitors' or adversaries' selfish motives for ministering—none of these mattered to Paul. Others would have to answer to God about their motives and methods, not to Paul. All Paul cared about was that the gospel was getting out there, and that's what it was all about, and that was enough.**

- **So what does this say about Christians who minister in ways you don't agree with? It may irritate you, offend you, may actually punish you—but if the gospel is getting to the people who need it, sometimes it just doesn't matter if you like how it's getting there. Sometimes doing a Christian task your way just gets in the way.**

About Christian death...

- **Even if getting the gospel out there spelled his death, Paul really wasn't concerned. Listen to what he writes—**

 For to me, to live is Christ and to die is gain. If I am to go on living in the body, this will

mean fruitful labor for me. Yet what shall I choose? I do not know! I am torn between the two: I desire to depart and be with Christ, which is better by far; but it is more necessary for you that I remain in the body.

- **Not that Paul had a death wish. He simply recognized physical death not as The End, but as a transition to a better mode of existence: to be with Christ! It doesn't get any better than that, he wrote. Yet he was willing to postpone his own pleasure (!) for the sake of Christians in Philippi and elsewhere who still needed him.**

Then distribute copies of **Wrong Motives, Good Deaths** (page 103) to all the students, get into small groups (preferably with an adult in each group), and let 'em start talking about the passage.

In the Book
[readers theater option]

Behind bars

stuff you'll need
- three students
- three copies of **Behind Bars** (pages 104-105), one for each reader

Use this **Behind Bars** (pages 104-105) readers' theater option if you want to explore the aspect of the *imprisonments of Paul*, springboarding from verses 12-14 in this session's Philippians passage.

Now I want you to know, brothers, that what has happened to me has really served to advance the gospel. As a result, it has become clear throughout the whole palace guard and to everyone else that I am in chains for Christ. Because of my chains, most of the brothers in the Lord have been encouraged to speak the word of God more courageously and fearlessly.

If you can, provide stools for the actors, although chairs will do fine, or the actors can stand if necessary. As with any readers theater performance—

- The scene is most convincing if rehearsed, even if it's read through only once or twice before your meeting.
- Try to choose actors who can read somewhat dramatically, interpreting their lines, not just reading them in a monotone.
- Actors should sit (or stand) in a row across the front of the room.

Notice that about 30 seconds into the script is a chance for your whole group to join the actors—at the part where Paul and Silas are in prison, "singing hymns to God"—by singing together a couple or three short songs that are familiar to your group. If you want to do this, decide ahead of time what songs those are, and prep your actors for them.

Closing

stuff you'll need
- one or two readers, each of them with a copy of **A Litany of Hope** (page 106)

Decide ahead of time if you will read the responsive prayer **A Litany of Hope** (page 106), or if a student reader will—and if you use *two* readers, they may want to alternate items. Then say something to this effect—

We've explored some dark, uncomfortable aspects of our faith—the question-

able motives of some Christians...what happens when a society's legal code permits the imprisonment of Christians just for being Christians.

Yet the Bible goes out of its way to remind us that there is no needless trouble, problems, or suffering—that, whatever or whoever you believe is the source of the trouble, God somehow, eventually, turns it all to good for his children.

After all, Paul doesn't say to the Philippians "Rejoice in the Lord always. I will say it again: Rejoice!" for nothing. He's in prison, they're suffering, problems on all sides—and the appropriate response, at least for starters, is to rejoice.

Let's close on that note right now.

Now call up the student readers, and instruct the group—

After each line of this prayer, respond together: "We will rejoice in the Lord always!"

Does God cause, control, or redeem trouble?

It is no secret that Christians disagree widely about the relationship of God and problems. We're not talking problems like trying to find a parking place in a crowded mall lot, but problems with a capital P—horrific tragedy, disease, victimization, abuse of all kinds, ethnicide—evil, plain and simple and stark. If God is God, what business does he have causing or even allowing such trouble?

Here's an extremely simplified, very general version of the subject (about which shelves and shelves of books have been written):

- On one side of this doctrinal teeter-totter are Christians who believe that God controls everything (though some shy away from saying God causes everything)—good, bad, and otherwise (how could an omnipotent God let anything slip by him?)—and that it's actually all good, and that it only appears bad or evil to us because of our limited perspective. In short, God causes (or controls) all things—what seems bad to us as well as what seems good— for our spiritual welfare.

- On the other side are Christians who believe that God can be God without controlling everything. These Christians are unwilling to believe that God is in any way responsible for the world's horrors—which are caused not by God, they point out, but by the fallen human condition, or sin. Yet they believe that there is no horror that God can't somehow redeem—no tragedy that God can't eventually turn to some good for his children. In short, God does not cause problems or tragedies, but redeems them for our welfare.

Of course, there is plenty of room on this teeter-totter to slide between and even beyond these two positions.

Good news of the gospel—or just goofy news?

As we'll discover a little later, St. Paul had a thing or two to say about motives and methods of sharing the good news of the gospel. (A clue—he was probably more tolerant than you are.)

Rate each of the following items—they're all absolutely true—according to how effective an outreach you think it is to non-Christians and unchurched persons, from 1 (not even Christian) to 10 (right on target). Simply mark (an X, your initial, a sketch of your pet, whatever—be creative) somewhere along the line to indicate your rating.

[newspaper article]

After the Preaching, Nashville Churchgoers Get Their Reward

NASHVILLE—A horde of faithful Baptists and some "backsliders" showed passes to off-duty policemen, proving they attended Sunday services, then crowded into a supermarket to buy half-price groceries as a reward.

"Some folks feel it was a gimmick to get people to church," said the Rev. Paul Durham, pastor of the Tadnor Baptist Church. "I confess. It was a gimmick."

But watching the crowd, which included some backsliders who had not regularly attended the church, he said, "This is a great success. I see lots of new faces here."

1 ———————————————————————— 10

Not even Christian	Tacky at best	Okay if you don't want to persuade anyone	Could work for a certain type of person	Right on target

[advertisement]

Church of Swing Dancing

A Full Gospel Family Fellowship * Paul Benton, Pastor * National Headquarters * Buena Park, CA

FIND GOD THRU DANCING...Every Sunday in "The Upper Room," Santa Ana, CA.

1 ———————————————————————— 10

Not even Christian	Tacky at best	Okay if you don't want to persuade anyone	Could work for a certain type of person	Right on target

[flier]

Interdenominational Bible Study

Mystery Questions of the Virgin Birth

- Was Mary the Mother of God?
- Did Mary keep a baby book on Jesus?
- Is it significant that "Santa" has the same letters as "Satan"?
- Did Jesus know he was the Messiah the day he was born?

1 ———————————————————————— 10

Not even Christian	Tacky at best	Okay if you don't want to persuade anyone	Could work for a certain type of person	Right on target

[newspaper article]

Winged—and a prayer

David Moore has created a truly updated edition of the Bible—it's bulletproof.

His pocket-size New Testament has a back cover made of Plexiglas and a bullet-resistant film that can resist a .38-caliber slug, he says.

Moore calls his $18.95 edition "God's Armor," after the passage in Ephesians 6:11, which says, "Put on the whole armor of God, that ye may be able to stand against the wiles of the devil."

1	Not even Christian	Tacky at best	Okay if you don't want to persuade anyone	Could work for a certain type of person	Right on target	10

[flier]

Try Something Unusual This Halloween

CHAMBER OF MARTYRS • NO ONE UNDER 12 ADMITTED

• Truth Stranger Than Fiction...Cruel, Macabre, Inhuman, but True!

• Dramatic Re-enactments of Those Who Gave Up Their Lives Rather Than Giving Up Their Faith

• Christian Challenge Center, Wednesday, October 31, 6-10 p.m. • Proceeds given to relief efforts for the Boat People

1	Not even Christian	Tacky at best	Okay if you don't want to persuade anyone	Could work for a certain type of person	Right on target	10

[advertisement]

24-Hour Telephone Answering Service

"Thou shalt call, and the Lord shall answer; thou shalt cry and He shall say, Here I am." Isaiah 58:9

Action Answering Service • Englewood, CO

1	Not even Christian	Tacky at best	Okay if you don't want to persuade anyone	Could work for a certain type of person	Right on target	10

[newspaper photo caption]

Confessional On Wheels

A priest identifying himself as Father Joseph of Carmel, California, pedals around New York City towing a portable confessional behind his bike. He calls it a "Portofess." THE CHURCH MUST TAKE A MORE AGGRESSIVE STANCE IN MEETING SINNERS, says the placard in his bike's basket.

1	Not even Christian	Tacky at best	Okay if you don't want to persuade anyone	Could work for a certain type of person	Right on target	10

[newspaper article]

Christian-gram an alternative singing surprise

If you can send a "Balloon-gram" for $25 or a "strip-gram" for $85, why not a "Christian-gram" for $30?

Such were the thoughts of Jack Jones, 19, the new president of the Dallas-Ft. Worth area's first religious singing messenger service, "Sweet Inspirations."

For $30 Jones' crew of two women and two men will croon your message anywhere in Dallas or Tarrant counties. They have prepared Christian songs for birthdays, get well, anniversaries, congratulations, and Valentine's Day.

But you get more than a message for your money. "For $30 we'll sing your message and give the recipient a heart-shaped brownie," Jones explained. "When we're through, we give them a New Testament and lead in a word of prayer."

1					10
	Not even Christian	Tacky at best	Okay if you don't want to persuade anyone	Could work for a certain type of person	Right on target

[classified ad]

Available to share true-life experiences with youth groups. Multidecorated Vietnam combat veteran walked point more than 250 times. Real-life experiences have inspired youth from coast to coast because this *Rambo* is Christ-centered. For speaking engagement, contact...

1					10
	Not even Christian	Tacky at best	Okay if you don't want to persuade anyone	Could work for a certain type of person	Right on target

[classified ad]

INVEST IN AN AMERICAN STUDENT. Hard-working Christian graduate of Syracuse demoralized by educational debt. Please help. Details: M. Vincent, Arnolds Bldg., 2792 Erie Blvd. East, Syracuse, NY 13224.

1					10
	Not even Christian	Tacky at best	Okay if you don't want to persuade anyone	Could work for a certain type of person	Right on target

All items from The Door (or The Wittenburg Door, an earlier titling of the same magazine). Sources in order of their appearance above: Apr/May 1982, Apr/May 1985, Apr/May 1985, Nov/Dec 1995, Dec 1984/Jan 1985, Dec 1980/Jan 1981, Jan/Feb 1993, Aug/Sep 1982, Jun/Jul 1986, Nov/Dec 1992.

News search–good, goofy, worst

- Best Good News
- Goofiest Good News
- Good News Achieved in the Worst Way
- Best Achievement by Worst Person
- Worst Achievement by Best Person

- Best Good News
- Goofiest Good News
- Good News Achieved in the Worst Way
- Best Achievement by Worst Person
- Worst Achievement by Best Person

- Best Good News
- Goofiest Good News
- Good News Achieved in the Worst Way
- Best Achievement by Worst Person
- Worst Achievement by Best Person

- Best Good News
- Goofiest Good News
- Good News Achieved in the Worst Way
- Best Achievement by Worst Person
- Worst Achievement by Best Person

- Best Good News
- Goofiest Good News
- Good News Achieved in the Worst Way
- Best Achievement by Worst Person
- Worst Achievement by Best Person

- Best Good News
- Goofiest Good News
- Good News Achieved in the Worst Way
- Best Achievement by Worst Person
- Worst Achievement by Best Person

- Best Good News
- Goofiest Good News
- Good News Achieved in the Worst Way
- Best Achievement by Worst Person
- Worst Achievement by Best Person

- Best Good News
- Goofiest Good News
- Good News Achieved in the Worst Way
- Best Achievement by Worst Person
- Worst Achievement by Best Person

- Best Good News
- Goofiest Good News
- Good News Achieved in the Worst Way
- Best Achievement by Worst Person
- Worst Achievement by Best Person

- Best Good News
- Goofiest Good News
- Good News Achieved in the Worst Way
- Best Achievement by Worst Person
- Worst Achievement by Best Person

- Best Good News
- Goofiest Good News
- Good News Achieved in the Worst Way
- Best Achievement by Worst Person
- Worst Achievement by Best Person

- Best Good News
- Goofiest Good News
- Good News Achieved in the Worst Way
- Best Achievement by Worst Person
- Worst Achievement by Best Person

Wrong motives, good deaths

First, read Philippians 1:12-26 aloud.
Then talk in your group about three or four of the questions below that appeal to your group. You may want to jot down some of your thoughts, or something that someone said that struck you as memorable or helpful.

About motives for ministry...

- What does Paul say about Christians who minister, but whose motives for ministry are wrong?
- Talk about wrong motives for otherwise good projects that you have seen or heard about. How easy or difficult was it for you to respond like Paul did?
- These verses talk about the wrong motives of others, to which Paul's response is "So what? The gospel's still getting out there, right?" But what if *we're* the ones with wrong motives? Is this a serious matter, or is it another "So what?" situation?

About death...

- If Hollywood agreed with Paul about death, how would movies be different?
- Where is there room for grief and sadness in Paul's otherwise cheery view of death?

About anything...

- Anything in these verses that's a puzzle to you? That just doesn't make sense?
- What one thing got your attention most of all in these verses? Why did it affect you the way it did?

Behind bars

A readers' theater of Acts 16:22-40 for three readers

If possible, actors should sit on stools across front of room. Chairs will suffice for a smaller group, or actors can stand. In any case, as is generally typical in readers' theater, actors in this scene do not leave their seats, but let their voices and upper-body language do the acting for them.

Notice that about 30 seconds into the script there's a chance for the audience to join the actors in "singing hymns to God"—two or three short songs familiar to your group. Decide ahead of time what songs those are and how you'll indicate to the audience to join in.

READER 3: The magistrates ordered Paul and Silas to be stripped and beaten, and the crowd joined in the attack.

READER 2: After Paul and Silas had been severely flogged, they were thrown into prison,

READER 1: and the jailer was commanded to guard them carefully.

READER 3: Upon receiving such orders, he put them in the inner cell

READER 1: and fastened their feet in the stocks. About midnight Paul and Silas were praying and singing hymns to God,

READER 3: and the other prisoners were listening to them. *(Here the Readers may sing a familiar song or two, inviting the audience to join them.)* Suddenly

ALL READERS: *(loudly)* there was such a violent earthquake

READER 3: *(also loudly)* that the foundations of the prison were shaken.

READER 2: At once all the prison doors flew open, and everybody's chains came loose. The jailer woke up,

READER 1: and when he saw the prison doors open, he drew his sword and was about to kill himself

READER 2: because he thought the prisoners had escaped.

READER 3: But Paul shouted,

READER 1: Don't harm yourself! We are all here!

READER 3: The jailer called for lights, rushed in,

READER 2: and fell trembling before Paul and Silas. He then brought them out and asked,

READER 3: Sirs, what must I do to be saved?

READER 2: They replied,

READERS 1 & 2: Believe in the Lord Jesus, and you will be saved—

READER 2: you and your household.

READER 1: Then they spoke the word of the Lord to him

READER 3: and to all the others in his house. At that hour of the night the jailer took them and washed their wounds;

READER 2: then immediately he and all his family were baptized.

READER 1: The jailer brought them into his house

READER 2: and set a meal before them; he was filled with joy because

READERS 2 & 3: he had come to believe in God—

ALL READERS: he and his whole family.

READER 1: When it was daylight, the magistrates sent their officers to the jailer with the order:

READER 2: Release those men.

READER 1: The jailer told Paul,

READER 3: The magistrates have ordered that you and Silas be released. Now you can leave. Go in peace.

READER 2: But Paul said to the officers:

READER 1: *(incredulously)* They beat us publicly without a trial, even though we are Roman citizens, and threw us into prison. And now do they want to get rid of us quietly? No! Let them come themselves and escort us out.

READER 2: The officers reported this to the magistrates,

READER 3: and when they heard that Paul and Silas were Roman citizens, they were alarmed. They came to appease them

READER 1: and escorted them from the prison, requesting them to leave the city. After Paul and Silas came out of the prison, they went to Lydia's house,

READER 3: where they met with the brothers

ALL READERS: and encouraged them.

A litany of hope

Responsive prayer

Two student readers alternate lines—or a single reader can read it all, or you can read it all yourself.

Ask students to repeat ***"We will rejoice in the Lord always!"*** *after each line you read.*

- Joseph told his brothers who had sold him into slavery and prison, "You intended to harm me, but God intended it for good to accomplish what is now being done, the saving of many lives." ***(We will rejoice in the Lord always!)***

- And we know that in all things God works for the good of those who love him, who have been called according to his purpose. ***(We will rejoice in the Lord always!)***

- Because we are confident of this, that he who began a good work in you will carry it on to completion until the day of Christ Jesus. ***(We will rejoice in the Lord always!)***

- For God comforts all who mourn, and provides for those who grieve in Zion—to bestow on them a crown of beauty instead of ashes, the oil of gladness instead of mourning, and a garment of praise instead of a spirit of despair. ***(We will rejoice in the Lord always!)***

- When people do the work of God without the spirit of Christ... ***(We will rejoice in the Lord always!)***

- When we ourselves fall into doing good things for selfish motives... ***(We will rejoice in the Lord always!)***

- When we face our own deaths, whether soon or later... ***(We will rejoice in the Lord always!)***

- When death takes us to Christ's side and we see him face to face... ***(We will rejoice in the Lord always!)***

(Everyone) **Amen.**

Bible verses adapted for this litany: Genesis 50:20, Romans 8:28, Philippians 1:6, Isaiah 61:3

Session 9

Bickering in the Back of the Church

Philippians 1:27-30
Philippians 4:1-3

During this session students will—

- Begin to distinguish valid disagreement from bickering when it comes to faith issues and relationships, especially with other Christians—and to be willing to put even valid disagreements aside when it comes to the work of the gospel.
- Understand how both *petty disagreements* and *suffering* can put pressure on a group's *unity*.

Inform your teaching

"Standing firm in one spirit" means knowing when disagreement becomes bickering.

Euodia and Syntyche are each mentioned only once in the Bible, and it's here in Philippians 4. And it's not the sort of context you'd want to be remembered in if

Don't think for a moment that Paul is reinforcing sexual stereotypes—you know, a pair of women cat-fighting, spitting and spiteful and ruining a church from the inside out with their tongues.

This is hardly the truth. First, these two women had been side-by-side with Paul, partners in ministry with him (verse 3)—and you can tell by Paul's language that they were still dear friends to him. Furthermore, Paul comes down a lot harder on men than he does on Euodia and Syntyche. Check out how, late in life, Paul veritably blacklists these males in his second letter to Timothy, his young protégé-pastor.

- "You know that everyone in the province of Asia has deserted me, including Phygelus and Hermogenes."
- "Demas, because he loved this world, has deserted me and has gone to Thessalonica."
- "Their teaching will spread like gangrene. Among them are Hymenaeus and Philetus, who have wandered away from the truth."
- "Alexander the metalworker did me a great deal of harm. The Lord will repay him for what he has done."

Compared to this, Paul's words to Euodia and Syntyche are a compliment.

you made it into the Bible. Basically, Paul begged these two women to *please* work through their disagreement and be at peace with each other—please, he wrote, "agree with each other in the Lord."

And in case they needed mediation, he called Syzygos, a Philippian man, into the fray, asking him to do what he could to help the two women iron out their difficulties.

So what do we know about this situation?

First, for what it's worth, Euodia's name means *fragrant*. Syntyche literally means *with fate*, and by extension *fortunate*. Not a big deal, but neat, huh?

Second, and more to the point, Euodia and Syntyche had been close ministry partners of Paul—they "contended at my side in the cause of the gospel," he reminds his listeners before they can turn and glare at the two women. Furthermore, scholars point out, Paul's plea to these two women leads off the hortatory section of his letter (chapter 4)—a prominence that suggests their disagreement really troubled Paul.

Hortatory? Eh?

It's just a theological term that refers to the parts of Paul's letters in which he exhorts his readers to do this or that. Very generally—and this loosely organized letter to the Philippians is not the best example of this—the first half of a Pauline letter tends to be doctrinal, and the last half hortatory. Often the hortatory part begins with a "Therefore..." or its equivalent—in other words, "Now that I've explained the ins and outs of what Christ has done for you, here's how your behavior should reflect this good news."

Third, the point of Paul's pleading with them isn't "Stop disagreeing!" as much as it is "Hey, people, you need to stand firm in one spirit."

Which sounds noble and biblical and all—but what did Paul mean?

It's pretty clear that he *didn't* mean that all the Philippian Christians should agree on everything. Certainly in the same church, then as now, conscientious Christians disagreed about all sorts of things—chariot speed limits on Philippi's streets...increased taxes for funding a new aqueduct...public school field trips to pagan temples.

What "standing firm in one spirit" *does* mean, if you take a broad view of the Bible, is that when it comes to the gospel, we ought to put our disagreements behind us—even if they're valid—so we can *together* put our backs into the work of the ministry.

Standing firm while suffering

In some ways, Paul expected a lot from his friends. This *standing firm* stuff Paul wanted the Philippians to do came in the middle of some sort of suffering, if we read between the lines of the last few verses in chapter 1: "Whatever happens, conduct yourselves worthy of the gospel of Christ...without being frightened in any way by those who oppose you...for it has been granted to you on behalf of Christ...to suffer for him..."

Although the Philippian Christians were subjected to dire, even suffering circumstances, Paul still held them to a high standard. "Live in such a way that you are a credit to the message of Christ" (1:27, *The Message*). Which may be one reason why Paul singled out Euodia and Syntyche: their conduct was anything but a credit to the gospel. *C'mon now, people, work with me—stand firm, be of one mind*, you can almost hear the apostle mutter as he pens the letter.

Standing firm, being of one mind, working cooperatively and peacefully for the kingdom's sake, even in dark times of persecution—this is probably the best defense against goofy, inappropriate, or downright wrong teaching slipping into the church. (authors' translation)

Opener [story option]

Aesop's fables

stuff you'll need
- a copy of **Tales from an Old Greek** (page 113) for each student
- pencils

Hand out **Tales from an Old Greek** (page 113) and ask students to follow the instructions: read each of the three ancient fables by Aesop, and supply an appropriate moral, or lesson, for each.

If your group is on the small side, you may simply want to read each fable aloud and discuss your way into a moral together.

If you divide into small groups for this activity, come together afterwards and debrief by discussing the morals and connecting each one to Paul's exhortations in Philippians.

Opener [active option]

Pressure cooker cards

stuff you'll need
- three decks of playing cards or equivalent for each group of four to eight students

Pressure Cooker Cards demonstrates the effects of pressure and stress—which represent "suffering"—on group unity. Assign your groups a task, then over the course of three minutes or so, add restrictions that undermine teamwork and community effort. The task can be anything whose completion gets tougher and then nearly impossible as you add more and more restrictions. We've chosen a simple card-deck-sorting task. Here's one way to do it—

FABLE	*POSSIBLE MORAL*	EQUIVALENT EXHORTATION IN PHILIPPIAN LETTER
The Four Oxen and the Lion	United we stand, divided we fall.	**Stand united, singular in vision, not flinching or dodging in the slightest before the opposition.** (1:27, *The Message*)
The Lion, the Bear, and the Fox	It sometimes happens that one man has all the toil, and another all the profit.	**Live in such a way that you are a credit to the Message of Christ** (1:27)**...I want the very best for you. Don't waiver. Stay on track, steady in God. Urge Euodia and Syntyche to iron out their differences and make up** (4:1-2). **Do you think Paul knew of this fable when he wrote to the Galatians, "If you keep on biting and devouring each other, watch out or you will be destroyed"?** (Gal. 5:15)
The Father and His Sons	Union is strength.	**This moral suggests Paul's hopes and fears for the church at Philippi: they were faithfully proclaiming the gospel, but somehow they had become disunited—two women especially were singled out. Paul understood that if they were not standing firm together, in one mind and spirit, the credibility of the gospel was at stake—not merely the survival of an organization.**

- If your group is larger than 10, divide into small groups of four to eight.
- Give each group three decks of playing cards or equivalent, thoroughly shuffled.
- Each group's task will be to sort the cards by individual deck, or by suit, or by number, or whatever you decide. If you want them to sort the cards by deck, make sure the three shuffled decks you give them all have the same backs on them—otherwise the task will be too easy.
- Make the activity a race between teams or against the clock—whichever best motivates your students.

Let's say you make it a race between teams. After students are in their groups and have been given their shuffled decks, instruct them along these lines—

First team to sort your decks by suit [or by number, or into individual decks, etc.] **wins. During the contest, I will add restrictions that you must follow. Ready? Go!**

After 30 seconds or a minute, say—

Whoops, now you can use only one hand.

After another 30 seconds or so, say—

Whoops, now only one person in the group can handle the cards—still with only one hand—while everyone else can only supervise.

After another 30 seconds—

Whoops, the card-handler in each group must work with closed eyes—no peeking!—and do as the supervisors say.

Then say—

Did I say sort by suit? I meant by number. Sorry...

If frustration gets serious, cut 'em some slack after another 30 seconds and let everyone join in, with both hands and with eyes wide open, for a dash to the finish line.

After the contest, debrief it with the students. Get them exploring the effects of stress on teamwork and community with questions like these—

As the restrictions started piling up—
- **Did some individuals in your group tend to take over?**
- **Did some people drop out of participating?**
- **Was there some disagreement in your group about how to go about the task?**
- **How else did the pressure affect you as a team?**

Segue to the next part of the session with words to this effect—

Living in such a way that the message of Christ is credible among unbelievers gets more and more difficult as pressure and stress increase—which may be one reason Paul had to remind the Christians in Philippi to stay of one mind: because of the stress of persecution on them.

In the Book
[object-lesson option]

Silver lining

stuff you'll need
- a glass bottle you can break into a clear plastic bag
- a piece of river-polished glass or machine-polished stone
- a copy of **Silver Lining** (page 114) for each student
- pencils, colored pens, or pencils

Use this object lesson to lead students to consider what happens to us when we follow God in our sufferings.

Before the students divide into small groups to work on **Silver Lining** (page 114), break the glass bottle (as dramatically as you can do it safely), then (carefully!) hold up one of the shards. Say something like—

Life can break us, shatter our dreams against rocks of death, divorce, disappointment, betrayal—just like this bottle shattered against the hard floor. Like these pieces of broken glass, we acquire sharp edges on our personality that can wound and tear. These edges can perpetuate the cycle of hurting among our family and friends—something like what may have been happening with Paul's two friends Euodia and Syntyche.

The way to beautify this piece of glass and make it safe to be around is friction. Over time in a rock tumbler, a rocky river, or on a stormy beach, this piece of glass will lose its sharp edges and produce a luster that appeals to beachcombers or collectors.

Show a piece of river-polished glass or a smooth river rock. As you talk, wet the piece so its beauty is more visible.

So it is with the kind of suffering Paul talks about in Philippians. The storms of suffering polish us and smooth us, wearing away our sharp edges. In that way suffering is a gift. The beauty we acquire from our suffering is the silver lining in the storm cloud of suffering.

Use the worksheet to record some of your struggles. Then determine what has been polished or made beautiful in life because you've trusted God through those struggles.

In the Book
[small group Bible-snooping option]

Here comes trouble...

stuff you'll need
- a copy of **Here Comes Trouble...** (page 115) for each student
- Bibles
- pencils

Now let your kids dig into the letter—specifically, Philippians 1:27-30—and explore in their small groups what Paul's instruction and encouragement means, and what it could look like in their own experience. Hand out copies of **Here Comes Trouble...** (page 115) to everyone, and save some time at the end if you want to debrief as a large group.

Closing

Prayer for Christians suffering today

stuff you'll need
- **Prayer for Christians Suffering Today** (page 116)—for you to read aloud, to photocopy and cut apart to distribute to small groups of students, or however you want to pray for these Christians.

Conclude with words to this effect—

As we've seen in this session, disagreement between Christians can be simply difference of opinion, or else it can get in the way of Christ's work in the church. And sometimes, as in the case of the Philippian church, Christians are unraveled to the point of losing patience with each other because of suffering—whether inner suffering or the persecution of their bodies.

When it comes to the persecution kind of suffering, first-century Christians have no monopoly on it. Then, Christians were crucified by Roman emperors and fed to lions in public arenas as entertainment. Now, the details have changed, but in much of the world the peril has never diminished, to this day.

Four of these five statements are true. Which one do you think is false?

1. **One-third of the world's people live in areas where preaching the gospel is restricted in some way.**
2. **More Christians have been martyred in the 20th century than in all of church history.**
3. **More Christians will die today than were killed on an average day in the Roman Coliseum—a Christian had a better chance against the lions in ancient Rome than she does today.**
4. **Every three and a half minutes, a Christian loses his or her life for belief in Jesus—that's 400 a day.**
5. **Two hundred million Christians suffer massacre, rape, brutal torture, beatings, mutilations, imprisonment, extortion, harassment, family division (children sold into slavery for the equivalent of $15 US), and crippling discrimination each year.**

Poll the group about which of the five facts they think is actually a fib, then reveal the answer: number 1. The truth is that *two*-thirds of the world's people live in areas where preaching the gospel is restricted in some way.

> The facts, names, and other details in this session's closing have been verified by Open Doors International, a leading mission agency helping the persecuted church around the world since 1955. This material is adapted from *Student Underground: An Event Curriculum on the Persecuted Church* (Youth Specialties, 2000).

Now use **Prayer for Christians Suffering Today** (page 116), profiles of three persecuted Christians in gospel-restricted countries. You can choose one to read aloud, and then pray for...or photocopy the page, cut the slips apart, and then distribute among small groups to pray for...or however you want to do it.

Tales from an old Geek

I stop, you stop, we all stop for Aesop. Long enough, at least, to read three of his ancient-but-oh-so-modern mini-tales and jot down what you feel could be a moral, or lesson, for each fable.

The Four Oxen and the Lion

A Lion used to prowl about a field in which four Oxen used to dwell. Many a time he tried to attack them; but whenever he came near they turned their tails to one another, so that whichever way he approached them he was met by the horns of one of them. At last, however, they fell a-quarrelling among themselves, and each went off to pasture alone in a separate corner of the field. Then the Lion attacked them one by one and soon made an end of all four.

Moral:

The Lion, the Bear, and the Fox

A Lion and a Bear seized a Kid at the same moment, and fought fiercely for its possession. When they had fearfully lacerated each other and were faint from the long combat, they lay down exhausted with fatigue. A Fox, who had gone round them at a distance several times, saw them both stretched on the ground with the Kid lying untouched in the middle. He ran in between them, and seizing the Kid scampered off as fast as he could. The Lion and the Bear saw him, but not being able to get up, said, "Woe be to us, that we should have fought and belabored ourselves only to serve the turn of a Fox."

Moral:

The Father and His Sons

A father had a family of sons who were perpetually quarreling among themselves. When he failed to heal their disputes by his exhortations, he determined to give them a practical illustration of the evils of disunion; and for this purpose he one day told them to bring him a bundle of sticks. When they had done so, he placed the bundle into the hands of each of them in succession, and ordered them to break it in pieces. They tried with all their strength, and were not able to do it. He next opened the bundle, took the sticks separately, one by one, and again put them into his sons' hands, upon which they broke them easily. He then addressed them in these words: "My sons, if you are of one mind, and unite to assist each other, you will be as this bundle, uninjured by all the attempts of your enemies; but if you are divided among yourselves, you will be broken as easily as these sticks."

Moral:

Your turn...

Now you write a fable with a moral. Let it begin like this:

A basketball coach had a team of the state's best and brightest players...

OR

On the afternoon shift at Burgerville was the fastest order-taker, the fastest burger-flipper, and the fastest deep-fryer...

Silver lining

You've probably heard people say, "Every cloud has a silver lining." Paul says as much, too, in his letter to the Philippians. Read Philippians 1:27-30.

One translation puts verse 29 like this—

There's far more to this life than trusting in Christ. There's also suffering for him. And the suffering is as much a gift as the trusting.

Think about some of ways you might be suffering for your faith in Jesus—or any other trials you may be experiencing. Pick one and describe it in the center of the cloud below. Then write along the perimeter of the cloud all the things you can be thankful for despite this trial.

MY STORM IS—

BUT THANKS TO JESUS,
I CAN BE GRATEFUL FOR—

Here comes trouble...

First, talk about this—

- *What are you most thankful for in your life?*
- *What is one of your struggles right now in your life?*

Now read Philippians 1:27-30, and choose one of the two following sets of questions ("What it means" or "What it could look like for you") to explore in your group. You may want to jot down some insights your group comes up with, or something memorable that one of you says.

What it means...

- Why do you think Paul says, "Whatever happens..." ? (1:27)
- Why should the Philippians "conduct themselves in a manner worthy of the gospel"? (1:27)
- How can the Philippians combat their fear of those who oppose them?
- What has the Philippians' belief in Christ also brought them? How so?
- How does it make you feel to know you might have to suffer for being a Christian?

What it could look like for you...

The following are quotes from the Philippians passages in *The Message: The New Testament in Contemporary Language,* by Eugene H. Peterson (NavPress). Read each one and write in specific details that further explain the meaning you take from the Scripture. First consider what it meant to the Philippians when Paul wrote it, and then consider what a correct response would be for you, your church, and your time.

- "Live in such a way that you are a credit to the Message of Christ" (1:27).
- "Your conduct must be the same whether I [that would be Paul] show up to see things for myself or hear of it from a distance" (1:27).
- "Stand united, singular in vision, contending for people's trust in the Message, the good news, not flinching or dodging in the slightest before the opposition" (1:27-28).
- "There's far more to this life than trusting in Christ. There's also suffering for him. And the suffering is as much a gift as the trusting" (1:29).
- "You're involved in the same kind of struggle you saw me go through, on which you are now getting an updated report in this letter" (1:30).

Finally...

- Anything in these verses that's a puzzle to you? That just doesn't make sense?

- What one thing got your attention most of all in these verses? Why did it affect you like it did?

Prayer for Christians suffering today

WU LING, China

Wu Ling is a traveling evangelist and Bible teacher. He has been imprisoned three times. The second time was for three years in a labor camp without trial. When Wu Ling was released, he defied the orders of the authorities and carried on with his preaching ministry. Now married to Sarah, he has a young daughter. In June 1997, Wu Ling was arrested a third time, placed in solitary confinement, and denied family visits.

Pray

- That God will protect him in prison and bring about his release soon.
- For travelling preachers in China who sacrifice time at home with family to serve their brothers and sisters who have no pastors or leaders. They put themselves at great risk to teach God's Word

AKHTAR YUSEFI, Iran

Akhtar lost her husband, Pastor Mohammed, in 1996 when he was murdered near their home in northeast Iran. Both Akhtar and Mohammed came from Muslim backgrounds. Since his death, Akhtar and her daughter, Ramsina, and son, Stephen, have moved to Tehran and are being cared for by believers there. Akhtar has struggled with her grief over the past few years but continues to seek fellowship and carries on in her walk with the Lord.

Pray

- For pastors, church leaders, and their families as they choose to stay in a country that threatens them with death if they attempt to serve God and preach the Good News.
- For Akhtar, Ramsina, and Stephen as they continue to deal with the loss of Mohammed.

ALI SALEHE, Tanzania

Ali is 17 and comes from a strict Muslim family. As the eldest son, he held a position of respect, and his parents had high hopes for him. But Ali became a Christian. When he told his parents about it, they kicked him out of the house. Ali was homeless and without a family but was determined to follow Christ. He was even rejected from school. Eventually a local pastor found him and offered him a home. Ali is trying to continue his education.

Pray

- That Ali will grow in his faith and be a passionate follower of Christ. Ask God to use him as a powerful testimony of love and forgiveness of his family.
- For other young believers like Ali who are forced to choose between family and their faith. Ask the Lord to give them a new family in the form of a caring Christian fellowship.

These names and facts have been verified by Open Doors International, a leading mission agency helping the persecuted church around the world since 1955. This material is adapted from *Student Underground: An Event Curriculum on the Persecuted Church* (Youth Specialties/Open Doors International, 2000).

Session 10

Blood, Sweat, and Tears—the Real Power

Philippians 2:1-3:1
Philippians 4:4-9

During this session students will—

- Recognize that although humility is slippery to define, we see in Jesus what humility looks like.
- Connect with peer experiences of humility and its opposite, arrogance.

Inform your teaching
What humility looks like

Humility drips from these sections of Philippians like sarcasm from Comedy Central.

The showcase passage is an ancient Christian hymn that Paul edits a bit and puts in his letter (2:5-11), a veritable hymn of humility to Jesus.

Your attitude should be the same as that of Christ Jesus:

Who, being in very nature God, did not consider equality with God something to be grasped, but made himself nothing, taking the very nature of a servant, being made in human

Lewis on humility

You won't find better or more succinct explanations of humility than in two books by C. S. Lewis, widely regarded as the single most influential Christian apologist of the 20th century:

- Letter 14 in *The Screwtape Letters.* If you are new to this book, the fictitious voice behind the letters is a demonic administrator in Hell's bureacracy.
- Chapter 8, "The Great Sin," in the section "Christian Behavior" in the book *Mere Christianity.* The sin, of course, is pride, whose opposite virtue is humility—both of which receive exquisitely clear explanations in very few pages.
- By the way, did you know that Lewis's initials stand for Clive Staples?

likeness. And being found in appearance as a man, he humbled himself And became obedient to death—even death on a cross!

Therefore God exalted him to the highest place and gave him the name that is above every name, that at the name of Jesus every knee should bow, in heaven and on earth and under the earth, and every tongue confess that Jesus Christ is Lord, to the glory of God the Father.

When it comes to humility, Paul wrote to the Philippians, Jesus was their example—so that they would "do nothing out of selfish ambition or vain conceit, but in humility consider others better than yourselves."

It gets deeper: "Each of you should look not only to your own interests, but also to the interests of others"—like Jesus, again, who put his own interests aside, instead taking on a human body in the great cosmic experiment called the Incarnation, God in flesh, the God-man.

Then there's Paul's request that the Philippians "do everything without complaining or arguing"—a test of one's humility if ever there was one.

Always giving

Next to Jesus, Paul spotlights the Philippian courier Epaphroditus as a truly humble person. After he had brought Paul his gift from the Philippians, Epaphroditus became almost fatally ill. Yet, Paul writes, he was not as concerned for himself as about the distress that news of his illness would cause back in Philippi! Plus he apparently waited on Paul hand and foot in his imprisonment, so that the apostle could write that Epaphroditus took "care of all my needs."

Paul himself shows a little humility, a little looking to others' interests instead of his own, when he offers to not only send Epaphroditus back to Philippi, but also to send Timothy, who "as a son with his father...has served with me in the work of the gospel." This was not an easy loss to Paul, who let the Philippians know that "I have no one else like him." But that was Paul, always giving and usually feeling giddy about it. "Rejoice always!" he seems never tired of saying in this letter.

You'll notice that the way Paul described it, humility looks a lot like passive resistance. For although you may have every reason to complain, argue, defend, vindicate—instead you submit, let yourself be "poured out" by God—much like libations, or sacrifices of expensive drinks, were poured out onto an altar to Yahweh or to pagan gods—and look out for Jesus' interests instead of your own. Humility is serving each other, and it's what unites us. It's the antidote to bickering and grudges (see the previous session) as well as to self-righteousness (see the next session).

It's all part of the paradoxical process that Paul wrote about in 2:12-13:

Therefore, my dear friends, as you have always obeyed—not only in my presence, but now much more in my absence—continue to work out your salvation with fear and trembling, for it is God who works in you to will and to act according to his good purpose.

Practicing a Christlike, Paul-like humility is just one way you "work out your own salvation with fear and trembling"—while at the same time acknowledging that "it is God who works in you to will and act according to his good purpose." This is a mystery, you chipping away at improving your attitudes even as you rest in the fact that God is doing his own good work in you.

Classic memory verses here

Finally, the verses from chapter 4 contain some of the most quoted passages in the Bible, possibly because they are such a hopeful mix of command and promise.

- "Rejoice always!" is the command, but you can do this because "the Lord is near" (verses 4-5).
- "Do not be anxious about anything, but ...present your requests to God" is the command, but you can do this because "the peace of God...will guard your hearts and minds" (verses 6-7).

If you or your students are in the memorizing mood, any of these verses (4:4-9) are downright inspirational to know by heart. In fact, the Philippians letter is full of such passages. Pick a couple and memorize them!

Opener [rating option]

(Quote) Humility is...(unquote)

stuff you'll need
- copies of **(Quote) Humility is...(Unquote)** (pages 122-123)
- pencils

Hand out copies of **(Quote) Humility is...(Unquote)** (pages 122-123) to students as they come in. By themselves or in groups they can read the list of quotations about humility and rate each quote according to how accurate a description or reflection of humility they feel it is. (By the way, if the third quote on the sheet, beginning "To be humble...," sounds familiar, it's probably because it's from the Bible—Psalm 51:17 to be exact.)

After everyone has had a chance to at least mark a few as their top choices, lead the group to share some of their choices and explain why they chose them. Then say—

Today we'll be adventuring through humility—at least what the apostle Paul writes about this elusive virtue. In an earlier session we learned that Paul wrote to the Philippians asking them to stand firm and be of one mind. In chapter two he seems to be offering his understanding of the one mind all believers should share—the mind of Christ. After recording what is likely the lyrics of an early Christian praise song about Jesus' humility, he describes what humility might look like and gives examples of two humble Christian men—Timothy and Epaphroditus.

Opener [poetry option]

Found poem

stuff you'll need
- a copy of **Found Poem** (page 124) for each student
- pencils

A *found poem* is so called because it is *found* in something written—a grocery store mailer, newspaper article, short story, anything—and arranged into lines, giving new and interesting perspective on the subject matter. For this exercise students will read the words of the hymn to Jesus in Philippians 2 and create a found poem to share with the group. See **Found Poem** (page 124) for details and an example.

In the Book [role-play option]

What does high school humility look like?

stuff you'll need
- four copies of **What Does High School Humility Look Like?** (page 125)

Rabbi Rafael of Barshad, a 19th-century European, summed up

humility with this story:

When I get to heaven, they'll ask me, why didn't you learn more Torah [the first five books of the Bible]? And I'll tell them that I'm slow-witted. Then they'll ask me, why didn't you do more kindness for others? And I'll tell them that I'm physically weak. Then they'll ask me, why didn't you give more to charity? And I'll tell them that I didn't have enough money. But then they'll ask me: If you were so stupid, weak, and poor, why were you so arrogant?

And for that I won't have an answer.

This story could describe the experience of adolescents who act as if they're omnipotent and invulnerable, even if intellectually they recognize their folly. Invite them to form small groups, distribute **What Does High School Humility Look Like?** (page 125), then say something like—

Sometimes it's easier to define a concept by understanding its opposite than by trying to contain the idea in a few words. The following exercise will help you picture how arrogance—and from that, something of how its opposite, humility—might look among your peers.

Read the parable at the top aloud. Then say words to this effect—

Now consider similar situations in your own experience here in [name your town]**:**

- **What sorts of things can a *lack* of humility lead teenagers here to do these days?**
- **What kind of humble response is appropriate after you've made an arrogant judgment?**
- **Better yet—what kind of humble response could you make *before* you act arrogantly?**

Brainstorm for a few minutes, then use your ideas to create a role-play of humble or arrogant actions typical of teenagers in this town.

Afterward ask some of the small groups if they're willing to do their role-play for the larger group.

In the Book
[small group Bible-snooping option]

Like-minded in humility and joy

stuff you'll need
- a copy of **Like-minded in Humility and Joy** (page 126) for each student
- Bibles
- pencils

Start the Bible study with words to this effect—

A story from the Jewish tradition tells this allegory of when God was preparing to give the Torah—the first five books of the Bible. All the mountains stepped forward and declared why they thought the Torah should be given on them.

"I am the highest mountain," said one. "No," said another, "I am the steepest mountain and therefore the Torah should be given on me." One by one, they all stated their claims. But in the end, God chose Mount Sinai—not because it was the tallest or the grandest (because it's not, as anyone who's toured the Sinai Desert will attest), but because, says the Midrash (a Jewish teaching text), it is the most humble.

Jesus' humility is what Paul focuses on as he exhorts the Philippians to right Christian living. Jesus himself taught us that he came to serve, not to be served—

and that was our example to follow.

Take the next 15 minutes to discuss the Scripture according to the questions on your worksheet.

Then distribute **Like-minded in Humility and Joy** (page 126). Afterwards debrief with questions like—

- **What happens in the youth group when we serve each other?**
- **What happens when we don't?**

Closing

Litany of humility

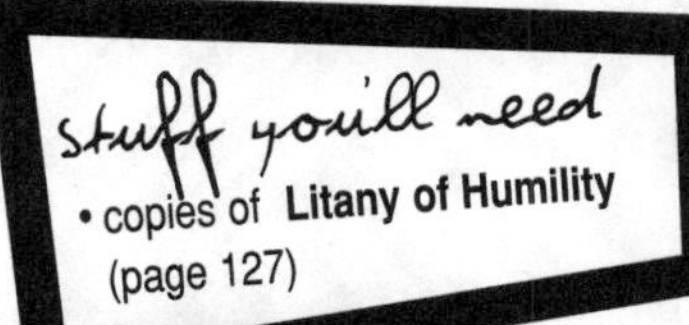
stuff you'll need
• copies of Litany of Humility
(page 127)

Bringing our casual, conversational ways to prayer can help when prayer needs to be demystified now and then. Yet the plainness of our vernacular just as easily robs a prayer or a confession of the solemnity it deserves.

As you read the **Litany of Humility** (page 127) responsively with your group, just flow with the formality of it. You or a reader can read it, while the group responds with the italicized phrases. Ask them to wait for a few seconds before responding with their part to give the words that you speak time to sink in. If they need help starting together, you may begin the response so they can join in unison.

(Quote) Humility is... (unquote)

Rate each of these quotes according to how well or accurately they reflect to you what humility means. Make your mark somewhere along the line, from 1 to 10, to indicate your rating.

Humility is when someone willingly puts himself last among his fellow-creatures.

1 ________________________________ 10

Doesn't describe humility at all to me | A fair description of humility, I guess | This is exactly what humility is to me!

The one who claims to be a searcher after Truth, who knows his limitations, who makes mistakes, who never hesitates to admit them when she makes them and frankly confesses them—this person is humble.

1 ________________________________ 10

Doesn't describe humility at all to me | A fair description of humility, I guess | This is exactly what humility is to me!

You can tell if you're humble only by comparing yourself to others who are also trying to be humble.

1 ________________________________ 10

Doesn't describe humility at all to me | A fair description of humility, I guess | This is exactly what humility is to me!

To be humble means have a broken spirit—a broken and contrite heart.

1 ________________________________ 10

Doesn't describe humility at all to me | A fair description of humility, I guess | This is exactly what humility is to me!

When we become aware of our humility, we've lost it.

1 Doesn't describe humility at all to me — A fair description of humility, I guess — This is <u>exactly</u> what humility is to me! **10**

Humility is the ability to be objective about one's own position in relation to everyone else. If I am in the position to lead, then I should lead. And if not, I should defer.

1 Doesn't describe humility at all to me — A fair description of humility, I guess — This is <u>exactly</u> what humility is to me! **10**

When I show by my somber attitude that I'm not fit for God, I'm at the beginning of humility.

1 Doesn't describe humility at all to me — A fair description of humility, I guess — This is <u>exactly</u> what humility is to me! **10**

Humility is devoting time and energy to God's work instead of one's own work.

1 Doesn't describe humility at all to me — A fair description of humility, I guess — This is <u>exactly</u> what humility is to me! **10**

If we could erase the *I's* and *mine's* from religion, politics, economics, etc., we would soon be free and bring heaven upon earth.

1 Doesn't describe humility at all to me — A fair description of humility, I guess — This is <u>exactly</u> what humility is to me! **10**

Humility is like underwear; essential, but indecent if it shows.

1 Doesn't describe humility at all to me — A fair description of humility, I guess — This is <u>exactly</u> what humility is to me! **10**

Found poem

based on a hymn to Jesus, Philippians 2:5-11

A *found poem* is a poem that—well, is *found* in something already written—a grocery store mailer, newspaper article, short story, anything—and arranged into lines, giving new and interesting perspectives on the subject matter.

Here, for example, is a found poem based on Abraham Lincoln's Gettysburg Address:

Fourscore and seven
new, conceived, and dedicated
all equal

a great civil war
a great battlefield
a resting place
fitting and proper

But
cannot consecrate, cannot hallow
little note, nor long remember
us the living
unfinished work, great task remaining
honored dead, not died in vain
government by the people
shall not perish from the earth

Now you write a found poem based on this hymn to Jesus in Philippians 2:5-11.

Your attitude should be the same as that of Christ Jesus: Who, being in very nature God, did not consider equality with God something to be grasped, but made himself nothing, taking the very nature of a servant, being made in human likeness. And being found in appearance as a man, he humbled himself and became obedient to death—even death on a cross! Therefore God exalted him to the highest place and gave him the name that is above every name, that at the name of Jesus every knee should bow, in heaven and on earth and under the earth, and every tongue confess that Jesus Christ is Lord, to the glory of God the Father.

Your found poem—

Invulnerability and omnipotence—not likely qualities in someone you feel is humble. Here's a parable that illustrates the foolishness of arrogant actions—actions that fly in the face of natural law, common sense, or deference.

> **Long ago, England was ruled by a king named Canute, who surrounded himself with courtiers who always praised him. They told him that nothing in the world would dare to disobey him.**
>
> **So the king asked the people if they thought the tide would stop coming in if he commanded it to stop. Oh, the tide would surely cease if you told it to, his courtiers told him. So the king brought his throne to the water's edge and commanded the tide to cease coming in. The tide, however, maintained its steady stream. The king became angry and cursed the tide and commanded it again to cease—but to no avail.**
>
> **And then the king realized that he may not have as much power as his courtiers believed him to have. Needless to say, they hung their heads and felt foolish.**

Now in your small group make up a modern-day parable of how humility (or it's opposite, arrogance) looks in your world, whether at home, at school, at a job, wherever—and be ready to role-play it for the large group. Use these questions to get you thinking—

- **What sorts of things can a *lack* of humility lead teenagers here to do these days?**

- **What kind of humble response is appropriate after you've made an arrogant judgment?**

- **Better yet—what kind of humble response could you make *before* you act arrogantly?**

The Canute parable adapted from http://www.pbs.org/adventures/Storytime/humility2.htm.

Like-minded in humility and joy

First, talk about this—
Do you think you would be a good maid, butler, or other service employee?

Now choose one of the following three Bible passages to read. After reading the verses, talk about the questions or statements that follow. You may want to jot down some insights your group comes up with, or something memorable that one of you may say.

Philippians 4:4-9

- Why is Paul telling the Philippians to rejoice?
- How should the Philippians handle trials and other things they're anxious about?
- What does Paul say will happen as a result?
- How is the peace of God described and how might it "guard your hearts and your minds in Christ Jesus" (verse 7)?
- Why should the Philippians think about the things listed in verse 8? How are these things related to the rest of this passage?

Philippians 2:1-11

- Why does Paul ask the Philippians to be "like-minded" (verse 2)?
- How does Paul say they can have unity?
- What does this passage tell us about the way Jesus lived?
- What did God do for him in return?

Philippians 2:12-18

- According to this passage, how else can the Philippians build unity through humility?
- Why would Paul want the Philippians to have unity?
- Who are Timothy and Epaphroditus, and how does Paul feel about them?
- What does it mean for us to be servants?

Finally...

- Anything in these verses that's a puzzle to you? That just doesn't make sense?

- What one thing got your attention most of all in these verses? Why did it affect you like it did?

Litany of Humility

Adapted from a prayer by Rafael Cardinal Merry del Val

O Jesus, meek and humble of heart,
Hear us.

From the desire of being esteemed, ***(deliver us, O Jesus)***
From the desire of being loved, ***(deliver us, O Jesus)***
From the desire of being honored, ***(deliver us, O Jesus)***
From the desire of being preferred to others, ***(deliver us, O Jesus)***
From the desire of being approved, ***(deliver us, O Jesus)***

From the fear of being humiliated, ***(deliver us, O Jesus)***
From the fear of being despised, ***(deliver us, O Jesus)***
From the fear of suffering rebukes, ***(deliver us, O Jesus)***
From the fear of being forgotten, ***(deliver us, O Jesus)***
From the fear of being ridiculed, ***(deliver us, O Jesus)***
From the fear of being wronged, ***(deliver us, O Jesus)***
From the fear of being suspected, ***(deliver us, O Jesus)***

That others may be loved more than us,
(Jesus, grant us the grace to desire it)

That others may be esteemed more than us,
(Jesus, grant us the grace to desire it)

That, in the opinion of the world, others may increase and we may decrease,
(Jesus, grant us the grace to desire it)

That others may be chosen, and that we may be set aside,
(Jesus, grant us the grace to desire it)

That others may be praised and we go unnoticed,
(Jesus, grant us the grace to desire it)

That others may be preferred to us in everything,
(Jesus, grant us the grace to desire it)

That others may become holier than us, provided that we may become as holy as we should, ***(Jesus, grant us the grace to desire it)***

(all) **Amen.**

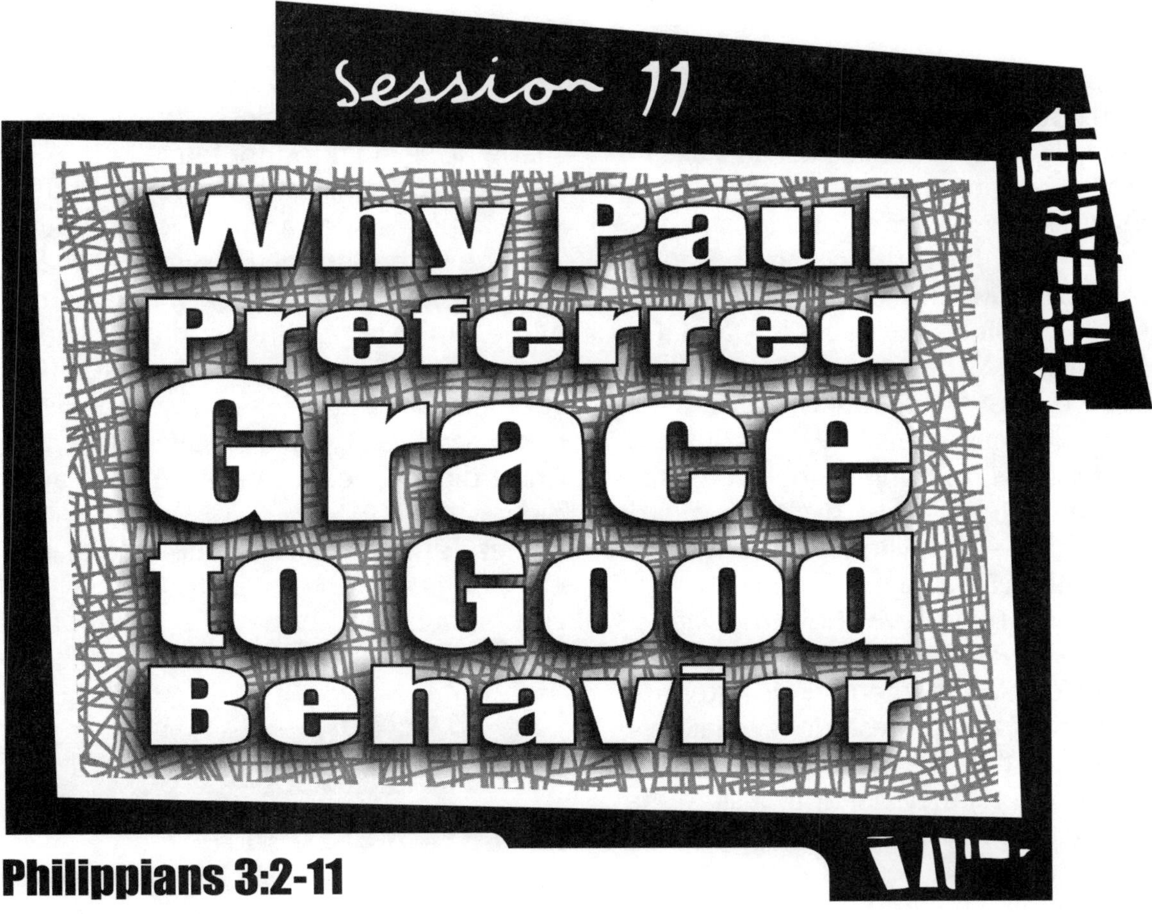

Session 11
Why Paul Preferred Grace to Good Behavior

Philippians 3:2-11

During this session students will—

- Recognize that Paul valued knowing Jesus Christ more than any achievement or position he might be entitled to in this world.
- Feel what it's like to be revolted by something another person finds appealing.

Nick the Convert?

You will be spellbound by this tale of grace and undeserved salvation to a raw and bitter pagan. You'll find it in *The River Why* by David James Duncan (Bantam, 1983), book 4, chapter 3: "Nick the Convert." Halfway through the chapter, start with the paragraph that begins, "We went inside." Of course, the entire book is a wallopingly frumptious read, with equal parts of the glories of fishing, the nuttiness of family, and Christian philosophy and religion.

You may even want to read this excerpt as the closing to this session. Give yourself 10 minutes or so.

Inform your teaching

Don't even try to earn goodness

Same problem as in the church of Galatia: teachers, whether from the outside or from within the church itself, were contradicting what Paul had personally taught the Philippians sometime earlier.

"Ah, yes, Brother Paul," says the wrongheaded teacher. "I'm sure he meant well about God handing righteousness to you on a silver platter. But he can't overturn two thousand years of Jewish teaching now, can he, just because of a very personal experience with God south of Damascus years ago? (Though many of us have our doubts about what really happened, if anything happened. You know how high-strung Paul is...he could have seen and heard anything out in that hot sun.)

"Anyway, it's as clear as the Torah here in my hand that to be right with God, you obey the Law of Moses. Simple as that. It was true for Moses and David and all the prophets, and it's true for us. No law, no salvation. So just because Paul gets all prickly about the ancient and holy Jewish requirement of circumcision, doesn't mean we can throw this commandment out the window. This is an eternal symbol of God's blessing to his people—and if us Gentiles want to be included in God's family, we must first follow God's law."

So when news gets to Paul about these teachers ravishing his beloved little flock there in Philippi, he warns his friends against them—and without mincing words, either: "Watch out for those dogs, those men who do evil, those mutilators of the flesh." Reminds one of Paul's excruciatingly logical statement in his letter to the Galatians about these doggy teachers: If these guys think so much of circumcision, Paul wrote, they ought to just go the whole distance and castrate themselves.

Elsewhere more serious in the Galatian letter, he wrote, "Mark my words! I, Paul, tell you that if you let yourselves be circumcised, Christ will be of no value to you at all."

So ya wanna compare credentials, huh?

Back in his letter to the Philippians, Paul got right in the faces of the Judaizing teachers. Fine then, he wrote, if this is all about being good Jews, just try to keep up with me—and off he goes into a recitation of his blue-ribbon Jewish pedigree (3:4-6), hereditary status and personal achievements that would make a wannabe Pharisee drool.

So by your standards, Paul wrote, I've got it made in the shade. But guess what? It's worth squat to God—and to me too, now. My high Jewish status, all my advanced degrees and fellowships and accomplishments listed under my name in Who's Who among Jews in the Eastern Mediterranean—it's nothing but dog poop to me now. (Really, that's the word Paul used—utterly useless animal excrement, not even good for fertilizer, the trashiest and stinkiest kind of rubbish that you simply want away from you, quickly, and the farther the better.) I've lost everything for the sake of Christ—I mean, look at me, I'm in jail and depend on friends like you for the simplest of necessities—yet I've never been richer, now that I've been accepted by God because of what Christ did for me, not because of what I did for him.

Yes, Paul would say to the false teachers, God is handing us righteousness—and salvation and hope, to boot—but on a bloody cross, not a silver platter.

Opener [object-lesson option]

To the highest bidder

stuff you'll need

- a substantial gift certificate for something your students would really enjoy, wrapped in a small box, and that box in a larger box

Place the large wrapped gift box—holding a substantial gift certificate for something your students would really enjoy—on a table in front of the group. Say something like—

Inside this box is a valuable item—really—which will go to the highest bidder. Because you didn't come tonight ready to bid hard cash, the bidding will be in the form of services. For instance, you may offer to [name things relevant to your circumstances like mow my lawn, provide babysitting in the church nursery, clean the van after our next trip, and so on]. **Let the bidding begin!**

You may have to convince them it's something that will be worth their efforts. ("This is not a trick auction, honest!")

Once you've heard a few bids, pick the "highest" bid (the one requiring the most work or sacrifice, perhaps). When the high bidder opens the gift—and here's your task—do your subtle best to elicit a reaction from the winner, preferably of gratitude and eagerness to use the gift certificate. (For example, if it's $20 certificate to a music store, ask what CD they'll buy...if it's a $30 certificate to a nice restaurant, ask who they'll take, et cetera.)

Then say something like the following—but make it appropriate to what occurred during your bidding—

You know what, you were such a good sport about stepping up to the bidding, that instead taking your payment of [say what they bid for the prize], **I'm waiving the payment. You may have it without doing anything more than you've just done!**

Okay, so your group was a bunch of skeptics who weren't willing to bid on something unknown—who suspected that, whatever the gift was, it wasn't worth their efforts. Or that it was merely a trick, and nobody wanted to risk being a sucker, regardless of how red in the face you got trying to persuade them otherwise.

This doesn't ruin the object lesson. If no one bids, or if bids are so low that they're not worthy of a $30 gift certificate, simply close the bidding. The gift has to be perceived as valuable before you can make the connection with the lesson. Unwrap the box yourself, read off the gift certificate, and then ask for bidding to begin. If you've chosen a gift with your group in mind, you'll get some responses. Choose the highest bid at any point in the process and give out the certificate. Then say your speech about waiving the payment and simply give the gift, free, to that bidder.

Make this observation—

It's only a small surprise to find out that you don't have to work after all to receive this gift certificate. But now let's talk about God's blessing of eternal salvation. Imagine your surprise—and even resistance—if, like the Jews, you were under the impression that you had to work to receive God's blessing, and then Paul comes along and says, "Never mind the working; God is offering you his blessing without you doing any good deeds but only merely receiving his blessing and using it."

Today we're going to read the part of Paul's letter that tells how even our best efforts are insignificant when it comes to earning God's approval... because God already gave us his approval through Jesus. (Keep in mind that Paul does not say work is useless; rather work that attempts to gain God's approval is futile.)

Is it faith or is it gambling?

Here's an interesting rabbit trail for those groups where no one was willing to work to acquire something unknown to them: Discuss how they perceive God's offer of eternal salvation. Yes, eternal life starts the minute you receive Christ, but we all know that the bulk of the gift will unfold latter—the redemption of our bodies, the restoration of the natural world, the ruling and reigning with Jesus. Obviously, we have no firsthand knowledge of that part of the gift. All we have at the moment is the cultural/church teaching that eternal life is desirable.

So how willing are we to change our behavior based on promises of an indescribably fabulous yet unknown future? How willing are we to obey Christ and follow the leading of the Holy Spirit if it means missing out on some earthly thing or experience we value? Do we receive Christ only to back down from full obedience because we're not convinced that the full unveiling of that gift in eternity is going to be worth the effort?

The gift is given. Are we on the way to the store to cash it in on eternal merchandise? Or are we so distracted by our present lives, SUVs, DVDs, and killer résumés that we've put our gift certificate through the wash cycle several times in the back pocket of our jeans?

Opener [skit option]

My achievements? Nothing but dog poop

stuff you'll need

- five copies of **My Achievements? Nothing but Dog Poop** (pages 134-136)
- four trick leashes that make it look like you're walking invisible dogs
- a plastic baggie
- brown Play-Doh

Let's be clear about this optional opener right up front: the skit on pages 134-136 is about poop. Dog poop, in particular. Subtitled "scatological yet scriptural," this skit is a graphic, humorous, and literal rendition of St. Paul's assertions in Philippians 3, where he writes that he counts all of his accomplishments as poop. The Greek word makes it pretty clear that Paul meant dog poop. Here's a case where the King James Version translates a word with gritty reality—dung—while most modern translations opt for a genteel translation: rubbish, refuse, or garbage. This skit is no impromptu affair...it will take a rehearsal or two to pull it off, but the effect is stunning. As long as you have a youth group that appreciates gross humor, that is.

Just be sure that the narrator reads the Bible passage to students at the start of the skit. Plus you'll want to remind them of the passage again afterwards. Facilitate a discussion in which kids can connect their gross responses to actors picking up the Play-Doh "dog poop" with Paul's feelings about any of his accomplishments compared to knowing Jesus and being embraced by him.

In the Book [small group Bible-snooping option]

Nothing compares to you

stuff you'll need

- a copy of **Nothing Compares to You** (page 137) for each student
- Bibles
- pencils
- optional: a testimony by you or another person

Hand out copies of **Nothing Compares to You** (page 137) to each small group. Give them 10 to 15 minutes to discuss the questions. Debrief the small-group time by inviting each group to explain one thing they learned. Then ask—

If a person actually believed that everything she could accomplish in this life is like poop compared to the "surpassing greatness of knowing Christ Jesus," what do you think her life would look like? In what way can you imagine a regular person like you or your friends living up to this image of a believer in Christ in the real world of home, school, work, relationships, personal development, and maturing?

This might be an occasion to give your testimony or to introduce another adult or student who believes that knowing Jesus is better than pursuit of any other accomplishment.

In the Book [hard questions & Bible-snooping option]

What did Paul mean?

stuff you'll need

- a copy of **What Did Paul Mean?** (page 138) for each student
- Bibles
- pencils

For more mature youth groups, you may prefer to use this Bible-study option.

Basically, it's hard questions about this session's Bible passage. Take a look at **What Did Paul Mean?** (page 138), and if it affords you some worthwhile directions for your small groups to go in, photocopy it, divide into small groups (or wrestle with it as one group, all together), and let 'em go. Be sure to debrief afterwards and provide some perspective if not hard answers.

Closing [symbolic option]

What is your greatest treasure?

stuff you'll need
- index cards or blank paper slips
- pencils

Hand out one 3x5 card to each student. Say—

Sometimes it takes a physical act to impress upon our brains a commitment we're making. That's why we have weddings and baptisms, for instance. So right now each of us will have a chance to commit to considering Jesus our greatest treasure.

Ask your students to write on a card accomplishments they are proud of. Say to them—

Look over your achievements, thinking about these things you treasure in life. Now close your eyes and ponder what Christ has given you—forgiveness of sins, a new identity as a child of God, and salvation by faith without you having to try and measure up to some legal standard.

If you choose to consider Christ your greatest treasure (not that your achievements are worthless, but that *compared to Christ*, if push came to shove, you'd choose Christ in a heartbeat—if you can do this, come and get a baggie. Wrap your accomplishments in the baggie and throw them in this trash. This symbolizes how you join Paul in considering all your achievements dog dung compared to the greatest gift of knowing Christ.

Closing [read-aloud option]

The short tale of Nick the Convert

stuff you'll need
- a copy of *The River Why* by David James Duncan (Bantam, 1983), book 4, chapter 3: "Nick the Convert." Halfway through the chapter, start with the paragraph that begins, "We went inside."
- a good 10 minutes in which to read this excerpt

If your kids like to be read to, and if you have the time, this tale will rivet them. It's a picture of grace and undeserved salvation that they'll remember for years.

My achievements? Nothing but dog poop

A scatological yet scriptural skit

Cast
- Narrator
- Shelly with her dog Beautiful Ballerina
- Trina with her dog Theological Seminary
- Seth with his dog High School Teacher
- Erik with his dog Powerful Political Office

Props
- four trick dog leashes that make it look like you're walking an invisible dog
- brown Play-Doh clumps
- plastic baggie

Setting
Shelly, Trina, and Seth obviously think their dogs' droppings mean something impressive. Erik begs to differ.

NARRATOR: The apostle Paul once wrote: We can't do the Lord's ministry by our own efforts, and we know it—even though we can list what many might think are impressive credentials. You know my pedigree: a legitimate birth, circumcised on the eighth day; an Israelite from the elite tribe of Benjamin; a strict and devout adherent to God's law; a fiery defender of the purity of my religion, even to the point of persecuting Christian; a meticulous observer of everything set down in God's law book.

The very credentials these people are waving around as something special, I'm tearing up and throwing out with the trash—along with everything else I used to take credit for. And why? Because of Christ. Yes, all the things I once thought were so important are gone from my lie. In fact, compared to the high privilege of knowing Christ Jesus as my Master, firsthand, everything I once thought I had going for me is as insignificant as dog dung. I've scooped that poop and dumped it all in the trash so that I could embrace Christ and be embraced by him.

SHELLY *enters on the left with* **BEAUTIFUL BALLERINA. TRINA** *approaches from center with* **THEOLOGICAL SEMINARY.**

TRINA: *(Talks to Shelly's dog in a high, cutesy voice.)* Hello, Beautiful Ballerina. How's the little lady today? Are you just dancing your little pads off these days? You bright little star of entertainment. You're just a few little prances away from the big time, little miss Beautiful Ballerina. I can tell. Yes I can. You're such a cutie.

SHELLY: *(Talks to Trina's dog similarly.)* Theological Seminary! You look so bright-eyed today. What a smart looking coat you're sporting for such a distinguished young lady. Haven't you just bowled over those old fuddy-duddy professors with your brilliance? Oh yes you have. Such a good girl.

SETH: *(enters left with High School Teacher)* Look, High School Teacher, there're your good buddies Beautiful Ballerina and Theological Seminary. Just in time for our lovely walk through the park. Let's go!

The three start walking. The next three speeches are ad-libbed because the three dog walkers are talking over the top of each other about training, study, work, and rewards of the various pursuits represented by their dogs' names. When they're into their ad-libbing, **ERIK** *enters left with his dog Powerful Political Office a few paces behind the other three. As* **ERIK** *gradually catches on to what the three are talking about, he keeps looking at his dog as if maybe he's missing something, because the others are speaking about their pets' achievements in such glowing terms.*

SHELLY: Dancing is so demanding. Practice, practice every day to improve, stay flexible, learn new moves. Oh, it used to be so simple, didn't it, Beautiful Ballerina? It was all classical ballet. I mean there are books written about it. You could study, do homework. Now the dance fads change overnight. Learning those modern moves while they're still in vogue is no picnic. But Beautiful Ballerina keeps at it—don't you, you good girl, you! One day this will all pay off. One day Beautiful Ballerina will reap the rewards reserved for those who give it their all.

TRINA: Going into the ministry involves so much more than mere Sunday sermons—doesn't it, Theological Seminary? There's all the practical coursework, certainly, like overseeing a church budget, providing leadership for elected church officials, knowing how to put together an effective worship service. Then there's the studies that separate the looky-loos from the serious students—things like New Testament exposition, the meaning and symbolism of the Tabernacle, the Reformation, hermeneutical science, and other equally unpronounceable words. And don't forget the liturgies for all the special occasions—weddings, funerals, dedications, baptisms.

SETH: No higher compliment can be paid to a teacher than a student who's excelled in school and graduated as a certificated teacher. Reproducing the heart of a learner and a teacher in children—that's where the rubber hits the road—isn't it, High School Teacher? Lesson plans, field trips, guest speakers, movie clips. Oh yes, keeping the students' attention is no picnic. One needs the likes of Julia Roberts, Brad Pitt, Gwyneth Paltrow, and the venerable Sean Connery to tackle education these days. Relevance, High School Teacher—you little stud, you! That's the key. How *does* all this math and English and history relate to the lives of high schoolers today?

Suddenly Beautiful Ballerina draws **SHELLY** *off the path as if she's sniffing around for a good place to do her business.* **TRINA** *and* **SETH** *stop dead in their tracks, watching every turn of* **SHELLY'S** *dog.* **ERIK**, *behind them a couple steps, also has to stop because the others are in his way, but he's watching the owners in wonderment and confusion.*

SHELLY: Just a minute everybody. *(In breathless anticipation.)* I think Beautiful Ballerina is going to *have an accomplishment. (The moving stops and* **SHELLY** *reaches down, cups her hand underneath where the dog's supposedly squatting and catches it—really slipping a Play-Doh log out of her sleeve and into the palm of her hand. She brings it up to her face and sniffs it. Ecstasy is in her face.)* Ohmigosh, it's...it's...a well-danced audition at Juilliard! (*She looks at everyone, giddy with elation. She sniffs the turd again.)* It's a scholarship! I just *know* it's a scholarship!

TRINA and SETH: *(screaming, hugging, celebrating with* **SHELLY***)* All right!...You *did* it!...I'm so happy for you...It's *beautiful!...(And more of the same.)*

SHELLY: *(She holds out the log to show her dog.)* Good job, Beautiful Ballerina. You did it! What an achievement! What a good girl! I knew you could do it.

In the middle of the celebrating, **THEOLOGICAL SEMINARY** *wanders off, apparently also sniffing for a good spot.*

TRINA: Look at this, will you? I think Theological Seminary is having an accomplishment, too. Good job, Seminary. Go ahead, sweetie, have an accomplishment. We've got all the time in the world. *(Everyone again watches raptly; you'd swear from their faces they were watching an Ice Capades finale.* **TRINA** *bends down to tend to the dog, inconspicuously drops a log of Play-Doh on the ground, and then picks it up to examine it.)* Look at this, would you? Straight As in New Testament Greek and church administration! *(More screams and hugs all around. They start walking again, each one ad libbing even more feverishly about their dogs and what accomplishments might lie ahead.)*

SETH: Hey, it's getting late—we'd better head back. *(They turn around and nearly bump into* **ERIK.***)*

SETH: Oh, sorry. I didn't know you were behind us.

TRINA: We would have asked you to join us.

SHELLY: You have a beautiful...*(looks at* **ERIK'S** *dog for the first time)*...uh, dog... What's its name?

ERIK: I call him PPO—Powerful Political Office.

SHELLY: *(with wonder)* Do you think when he has an accomplishment, it could be, like, president of the United States or something?

ERIK: *(cringing)* I dunno...I suppose so...

SETH: Oh look—he's sniffing around.

ERIK *is nonplussed about the process.* **PPO** *squats.* **ERIK** *sort of turns his head and wrinkles his nose at the stinky process. The other three have their eyes glued on* **PPO**, *ready to pounce on the results of the dog's efforts so they can see what its* accomplishment *is.*

TRINA: It *could* be the presidency, although I've never smelled that accomplishment up close.

SETH: No, I think it's victory in a senatorial race.

SHELLY: Whatever it is, it's really a big one.

ERIK *looks at the three other dog owners with incredible revulsion on his face—just as his leash moves away from the spot. The three watch with anticipation as* **ERIK** *reaches into his pocket and pulls out a baggie. As he reaches down to the spot, he secretly releases a couple of Play-Doh logs on the floor, then picks them up in the plastic bag, obviously trying not to touch them.)* Yuck. I hate this part. *(He gingerly ties off the bag or seals it.* **SHELLY, TRINA,** *and* **SETH** *are aghast.)*

SETH: What are you doing?

ERIK: Uh, sorry...is there a trash can around here? PPO and I are on our way to meet Jesus, and I wouldn't want to be carrying this dog poop in my pocket when he greets me with a hug.

END

Nothing compares to you

First, talk about this—

- *What is the most valuable thing in your life?*
- *Why is it valuable?*

Now choose one of the two passages, and read it. Then talk about the questions or statements that follow. Jot down some of your thoughts or something memorable that one of you may say.

Philippians 3:2-6

- Who are the "dogs, those men who do evil, those mutilators of the flesh"? (verse 2) Why does Paul call them that?
- Why does Paul call the Philippians "the circumcision"? (verse 3)
- How might Paul or anyone else "put confidence in the flesh"? (verse 4) Why does Paul say he has more reason to put confidence in the flesh?

Philippians 3:7-11

- What does Paul think of all his achievements now? Why?
- From where did Paul formerly believe he gained his righteousness? From where does he gain it now and how?
- What is the result of his new knowledge?
- Why does Paul say he wants to share in Christ's sufferings?
- How might Paul become like Christ?

Finally...

- Anything in these verses that's a puzzle to you? That just doesn't make sense?

- What one thing got your attention most of all in these verses? Why did it affect you like it did?

WHAT DID PAUL MEAN?

HARD QUESTIONS IN PHILIPPIANS 3

Have someone in your group read St. Paul's letter to Christians in Philippi, chapter 3 verses 2-11 aloud.

- Say you don't have a background like Paul's—no impressive list of things that you were born into or achieved. Does that mean it may actually be easier for you than it was for Paul to accept God's gifts? What light do Jesus' words in Luke 18:18-25 shed on this question?

- A lot of people are put off by Paul because at first reading, he comes across as so black and white—at least in the letters he writes. To such people, this passage is an example of that: whatever was once a credit to Paul, he discounts it as dog poop (which is what the Greek word actually suggests—*rubbish* just doesn't do justice to Paul's intensity)—worthless, stinky, not even good for fertilizer. Just toss it, the sooner and farther away the better.

  So what is Paul recommending here? That you gather however many or few accomplishments you've achieved (high GPA...first string soccer team...a job you worked hard to get, that pays well more than minimum wage) or benefits you've inherited (good looks...natural talent...a two- or three-car family that can buy you pretty much what you want without straining the budget)—and walk away from them? Deny them? Throw them away? As noble as Paul's recommendations sound, wouldn't most people call you ungrateful and irresponsible if you did what he said? Talk about this.

- What other conflicting feelings do you have about being asked to treasure Christ more than anything else? Is this practical? What does this look like in today's world?

- In what ways did Paul demonstrate that he treasured Christ more than anything else? Could you imitate any of these ways if you wanted to? Which ones? How?

- Spend a few minutes with these historical people who demonstrated their love and desire for God more than anything else (and do we mean *anything*):

  —A patriarch. Genesis 22:1-13
  —A mother. 1 Samuel chapter 1
  —A whore. Luke 7:36-50 and Matthew 26:6-13

  Could you imitate any of these acts of love? Do you think God wants you to?

- Write a letter to Paul about why a student today could be expected to actually treasure Christ above all else. Or *to what degree* a student today could do this. Or why a student today could *not* do this.

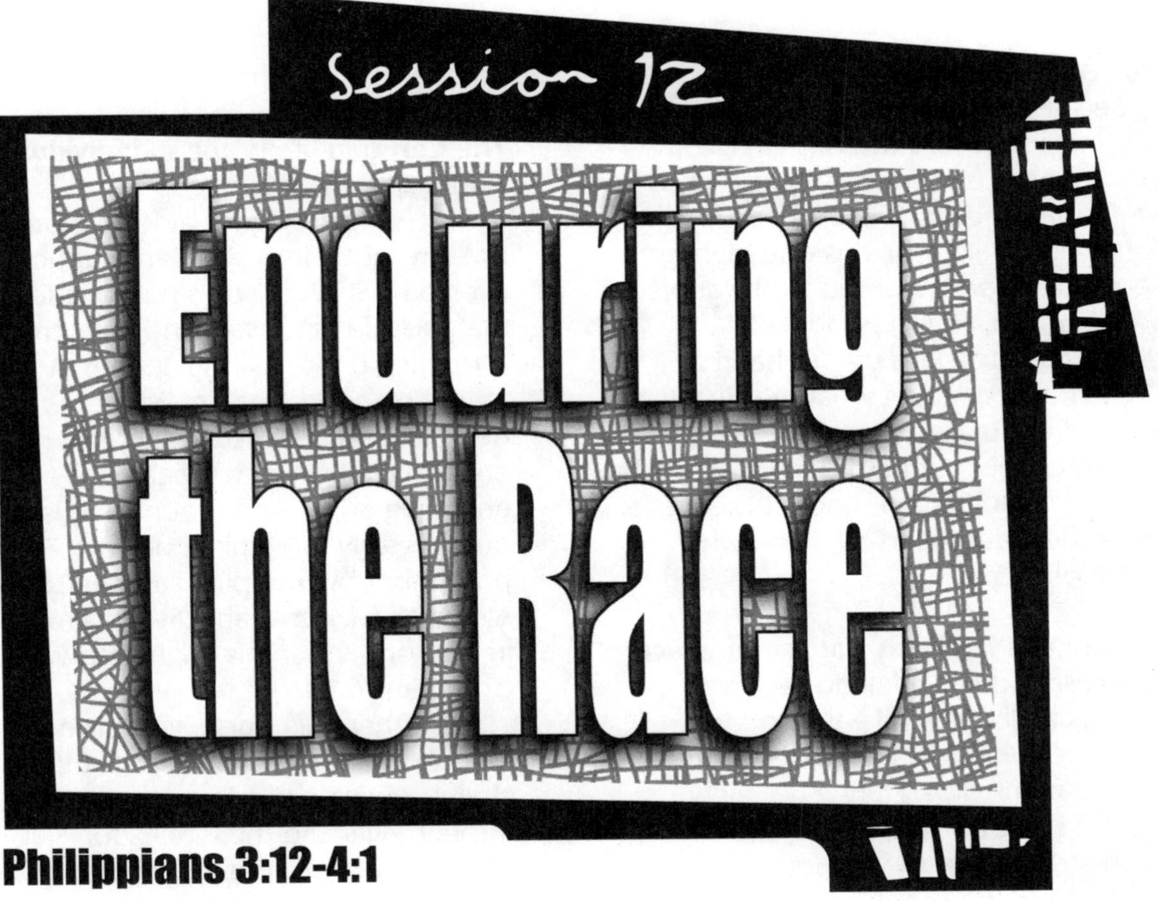

Session 12: Enduring the Race

Philippians 3:12-4:1

During this session students will—

- Understand the place that the trait of endurance has in a Christian's life.
- Connect God's promises with the their own dilemmas.

Inform your teaching

What Christian endurance isn't

In this classic Bible passage, Paul borrows the image and language of stadium races during his day. "Straining toward what is ahead," he wrote, "I press on toward the

Endurance in popular media

Looking for some extra-biblical examples of endurance? You won't have to look far—literature and movies are full of them, most of them suitable to use somewhere in this session to give your kids yet another spin on this subject. Maybe one of these may work for your group:

- Any story about a quest, whether in print or on video, inevitably contains scenes that depict the consequences both of enduring and *not* enduring. Take *Star Wars: The Empire Strikes Back*—Luke's inability to follow through with his training under Yoda leads him by the nose right into Darth Vader's trap. Or the climax of The Lord of the Rings, when Frodo's endurance finally evaporates in his struggle against the Ring's power, and at the last moment he succumbs to—well, if you've read it, you know what he succumbs to. (If you, the youth leader, haven't read it, start now. In the process, you'll collect years' worth of youth talk illustrations.)
- In *Forrest Gump* are several examples of endurance: quite literally, his coast-to-coast run as a means of coping with Jenny's departure...his patient endurance of his Vietnam lieutenant's bitterness...even Jenny's near-suicide scene is something of an inside-out instance of endurance, in that fear (or something) kept her hanging on to life a little longer.
- Or pick a scene with a similar endurance theme from a favorite book of yours that will connect with your kids, whatever their tastes—something from Harry Potter, Tom Clancy, the Left Behind series, whatever.

goal to win the prize..."

Because a foot race is a particularly vivid metaphor for the Christian life, it's been used a lot by writers and preachers and speakers. And like any metaphor, this one highlights only *some* features of the subject, not all. So like good Bible exegetes, let's try our hand at understanding what the Christian race and endurance are in the context of the entire Bible. Furthermore, let's do it by process of elimination, since some things can be best described by listing what they're *not.*

Exegesis is the critical explanation or analysis of a text.

- **The Christian life is not just one race**, unless you consider life itself a race. It's actually more like the Tour de France, which is raced in 20-some legs in as many days. During the nights between their racing days, cyclists enjoy sit-down meals, hot showers, and clean beds. Yet the 2000-plus-mile race is considered by some to be the world's most strenuous and mentally and physically demanding athletic contest.

  Similarly, your pressing on toward a goal has periods or seasons of relative rest between legs of your race, whatever your race happens to be.

- **Endurance is not maintaining 110 percent effort all the time**—contrary to much Bible exhortation aimed especially at adolescents. As if such a sustained effort is even possible. The only reason people can exert even 80 percent effort for any length of time is because they've trained and rested. The idea of Christians *never* letting down and simply *being* once in a while is not a biblical teaching. It's not even common sense. And the people in this world who never let down aren't necessarily more spiritual—they're simply Type A. Which is fine. But which is not for everybody.

- **The Christian life is not an individual event.** If you want to keep the footrace metaphor, it's at least more like a relay. Or let's switch metaphors: even a NASCAR driver is part of a team that includes sponsors and a pit crew. A running back has his linemen. A magazine editor has her writers, designers, fact-checkers, and advertisers. The Bible, in fact, repeatedly encourages us *not* to count on just ourselves. "Not by might nor by power, but by my Spirit, says the Lord Almighty..." (Zechariah 4:6) "Be strong in the Lord and in his mighty power" (Ephesians 6:10).

  And then, of course, you have the New Testament teachings about the church. Doing a quick read straight through Acts and the letters, for example, you get the feeling that conversion to Christ pretty much means conversion to other Christians in your neighborhood. Not that Christians were meant to live in a Christian ghetto—indeed, much of being a Christian is to live in the larger world, among unbelievers, as light and salt (instead of behavior sheriffs or, worse, judges). It's only that, somehow, the church should be as peculiar and welcoming and gracious a witness to the power and love of God as an individual Christian should be. It's an ongoing, fluid, two-way process—the work God does in you is needed by the church, and *you* need the work God does in the church.

  A quick word to youth workers, who for a number of reasons often have fewer peer friends than others: sooner or later, you'll need a couple *good* friends. So if you don't have some, start investing yourself in them now. Life being what it is, you simply *can't* endure some of life's races by yourself. Period. There will come a time when neither students nor coworkers can help you, a time when you won't need cheerleaders and admirers, but peers with whom you have some shared history.

- **Enduring the Christian race does not necessarily mean you always have the goal in sight.** Again, if you're talking about the race being this life, of course, then physical death or seeing Christ face to face could be called the goal. (Although we will probably be surprised when we see him in those circumstances. What we thought until then would be the goal will seem to us, perhaps, as only the beginning of something else entirely.)

  But during some legs of this race, it's not unusual to lose sight of the goal altogether. Now and then we will even lose sight of why we're running in the first place, doubting the very necessity of the race. At such times, if we've done our work, training will kick in, and our legs will keep pumping even when we're arguing with ourselves or with God. And there's another reason the church is important to us: those seasons in which we would give up if left to our own reasoning, but for the coaching and encouraging we receive from the sidelines. In *The Screwtape Letters* C. S. Lewis implies that our rote obedience during such times of doubt and stumbling may be the sweetest, most convincing kind of obedience God sees in us:

  > *[God] wants them to learn to walk and must therefore take away His hand; and if only the will to walk is really there He is pleased even with their stumbles. [Hell's] cause is never more in danger than when a human, no longer desiring, but still intending, to do [God's] will, looks round upon a universe from which every trace of Him seems to have vanished, and asks why he has been forsaken, and still obeys.*

Now on to encouraging your students to endure their own races, whatever kind of races they are.

Opener [game option]

Soda stacks

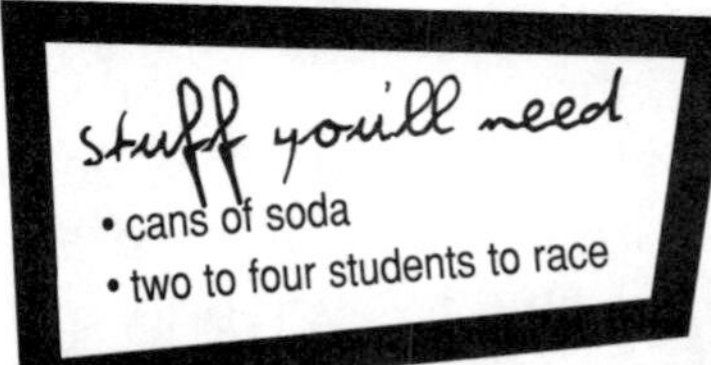
stuff you'll need
• cans of soda
• two to four students to race

This **Red Light/Green Light** game illustrates unexpected grace in what racers thought would be a highly competitive contest—in this race, you're not on your own.

Send your racers from the room to get what they need for the race. At least that's why they *think* they're leaving the room. You actually want them out of earshot. Here's why.

While the competitors are each getting an armful of full, unopened cans of soda elsewhere in the building, you tell the group that the competitors will be given these rules—

1. Competitors will race from a starting line to a finish line, moving only when the leader says "Green light!" and stopping when the leader calls "Red light!"—and they each race with an impossibly tall stack of full, unopened cans of soda in each hand.
2. If they drop any cans, competitors must stop right there, put down their stacks, rebuild their stacks, pick them up, then continue toward the goal. The leader does *not* have to wait for them to pick up their sodas before calling the next "Green light!"

3. Competitors will be told that the race is highly competitive.
4. Furthermore—*and this is critical*—tell the competitors that the group as spectators can do anything they want to the racers—within reason, of course—and the racers *can't* object.
5. Finally, at the conclusion of the race, all racers must drink the top can—the can presumably most likely to have been dropped and shaken.

So much for the rules as the *competitors* will hear them. Here's what you tell the group while the competitors are out of the room: Whenever a racer drops a can, spectators should rush to pick up the can and replace it *for* the racer, so the racer can quickly continue.

Furthermore, tell the group that, when the competitors return to the room and you read rules 1 through 5 to everyone, the group should react to the rules as if they're hearing them for the first time, as the competitors are. (Some bloodthirsty reactions are appropriate when rule 4 is read!)

So...when competitors return to the room with their sodas, tell everyone rules 1 through 5 above—and let the race begin! The soda stacks should be tall enough to be inevitably toppled by most people at least a couple times. When the race is over—and the competitors are astounded by the help they got—add this final grace note: instead of making them drink the top soda on their stack and probably getting sprayed by it in the process, reveal some private, short stacks of cold sodas there in the room—and give them each a "top" soda they can drink in peace.

Segue to the next part of this session with words to this effect—

We're used to races being cutthroat, competitive affairs. The race that St. Paul alludes to in this week's Bible passage is way different. For starters, the race of life isn't an individual event as much as it is a team event. And that team can be, for this season of your life, good friends, family members, this youth group, or another group that knows you and loves you.

Because the race you're in or will inevitably be in—to get accepted to the job or college you want....to *keep* that job or stay in that college...to push through a tough season in a relationship...to endure any short-term or long-term pressure or strain—these are races of endurance that the Bible gives you a lot of hope for and a lot of help with.

Opener
[small group discussion]

And in lane three...YOU!

> stuff you'll need
> • a copies of **And in Lane Three...YOU!** (page 144) for each student or for each small-group leader

Give each student or each small-group leader a copy of **And in Lane Three...YOU!** (page 144). Ask them to spend five to 10 minutes talking about those questions that particularly interest them. If you want, debrief together as a large group afterwards.

In the Book
[small group discussion]

Running the race: case studies

> stuff you'll need
> • a copy of **Running the Race: Case Studies** (page 145) for each student

Here's a discussion starter to kick off with something like—

Meet some people like you, each of whom has his or her own race.

Then hand out copies of **Running the Race: Case Studies** (page 145), read aloud this sheet's intro (everything down to the first case study, "Deanna"), then release the kids to explore the cases among themselves.

In the Book
[small group Bible-snooping option]

Christian marathon

stuff you'll need
- a copy of **Christian Marathon** (page 146) for each student
- Bibles
- pencils

Say something like this—

This week's Bible passage contains some of the New Testament's most quotable and preached-on snippets—

- **"Forgetting what is behind...straining toward what is ahead...I press on toward the goal..."**
- **"Our citizenship is in heaven."**
- **"Stand firm in the Lord!"**

But they're more than snippets—as you'll see as you explore this part of Paul's letter to his close friends in Philippi.

Then distribute **Christian Marathon** (page 146) to all your students, assign small groups if you want, and let them take off. After-wards, debrief each other in the larger group if you want.

Closing [diagram option]

Tour de Life

stuff you'll need
- a copy of **Tour de Life** (page 147) for each student
- pencils

For those of you who aren't up on cycling, here are some details that are not only fascinating in their own right, but provide a segue to the closing activity, **Tour de Life** (page 147)—

With back-to-back wins in 1999 and 2000, Lance Armstrong became only the second American, and the first with an American team, to win cycling's show-case race, the Tour de France—an annual 2000-plus-mile bicycle race that winds around the entirety of France—including up some unbelievable inclines in France's mountains. What made news more than Armstrong's nationality was the fact that he won his first title less than three years after being diagnosed with testicular cancer that spread to his brain and lungs. Doctors had given him only about a 50 percent chance of survival.

Closing [listening option]

The finish line

stuff you'll need
- a CD or tape of the Steve Taylor song "The Finish Line," on the album *Squint*
- a boom box
- a copy of **The Finish Line** lyrics (page 148) for each student

If you're familiar with Steve Taylor's song "The Finish Line" on the album *Squint*, you'll immediately recognize it as the perfect close to a session on endurance in the Christian race. It's a perfect benediction. If you don't know it, give it a listen and decide for yourself. You may want to open this session rather than close it with the song. Your call.

And in lane three...YOU!

- What's felt like a race to you recently?
- Does it feel more like a sprint or a marathon?
- What stumbles or falls have you made in this race?
- What help from outside yourself have you been offered? Did you receive it? Why or why not?

And in lane three...YOU!

- What's felt like a race to you recently?
- Does it feel more like a sprint or a marathon?
- What stumbles or falls have you made in this race?
- What help from outside yourself have you been offered? Did you receive it? Why or why not?

And in lane three...YOU!

- What's felt like a race to you recently?
- Does it feel more like a sprint or a marathon?
- What stumbles or falls have you made in this race?
- What help from outside yourself have you been offered? Did you receive it? Why or why not?

And in lane three...YOU!

- What's felt like a race to you recently?
- Does it feel more like a sprint or a marathon?
- What stumbles or falls have you made in this race?
- What help from outside yourself have you been offered? Did you receive it? Why or why not?

Running the race: case studies

Listen to what Paul wrote to his friends in Philippi—

One thing I do: Forgetting what is behind and straining toward what is ahead, I press on toward the goal to win the prize for which God has called me heavenward in Christ Jesus.

There's far more to life for us. We're citizens of high heaven! We're waiting the arrival of the Savior, the Master, Jesus Christ, who will transform our earthy bodies into glorious bodies like his own. He'll make us beautiful and whole with the same powerful skill by which he is putting everything as it should be, under and around him. (Chapter 3, verses 13-14, 20-21, *The Message.*)

Below are stories of the kinds of people you know—people in your neighborhood or town—or maybe they're *your* stories, or the stories of the person you may become one day. Not famous, not movers and shakers. Just normal people in the daily grind.

Choose one of the stories that interests you, and explore in your small group how the story could resolve if that person lived with the attitude Paul talked about above. Would the story necessarily have a happy outcome? What shape would "the prize" take if that person persevered toward God's goal? Would Paul's message be encouraging to that person or not? Why?

Talk about this, and be ready to explain your story ending to the larger group.

Deanna, department of motor vehicles employee
"All the people who come into the DMV are rude. Whether it's teenagers or older adults, they're so stressed about taking tests and standing in line that they end up being rude to me. It makes my job so hard—I go home angry or depressed every day!"

Tom and Marcia, newlyweds
"Getting started takes both of us working. We're waiting to have kids until we have a house and a little savings so one of us can be the stay-at-home parent. We're planning to be involved in church, but right now we need Sundays for ourselves just to unwind from the week."

Kalim, high school junior—college prep
"The academic pressure at my school makes us all anxious to do well—even when our home schedules keep us from studying like we know we should. My friend's parents are fighting tonight and are talking separation. She called to say she just can't study and asked if I would place tomorrow's English test paper on the side of my desk so she can check any answers she's uncertain about."

Jenny, widow
"It's not like my husband was my life. I've always had the kids to be there for—two are still at home—and taught my community ed classes. But it's like my face feels heavy all the time. It's such an effort to smile, much less laugh. An out-of-the-blue accident like that makes you unwilling to believe you'll ever be safe again."

Juan, retired
"It's been lonely around the nursing home. The people who work here are nice, but they're so busy that they don't really have time to sit and talk. My family lives in another state, so they can't visit very often. If I have to go on living like this, I think I'll lose my mind."

Brian, unemployed father of two
"I haven't been able to find a job since I was laid off a year ago. My family has lived on welfare and under-the-table payments for odd jobs I can get. Groceries, rent, and basic necessities use that up each month. My folks have been good enough to pay for the kids sports this fall. I feel like I'm letting my family down."

CHRISTIAN MARATHON

First talk about this—

- *What do you know about marathons—the training methods, techniques for running, goals (think of various goals that different kinds of runners have), obstacles?*
- *Why do you think people go to all the trouble of training for and running marathons?*

Now choose one of the three passages below, and read it. Then talk about the questions or statements that follow. Jot down some of your thoughts or something memorable that one of you may say.

PHILIPPIANS 3:12-14

- What is the feeling or mood of this passage?
- Why does Paul press on?
- What are Paul's goals?
- Why does he call the Christian life and heavenly reward a "prize"?

PHILIPPIANS 3:15-20

- Why does he say those who are mature would have "such a view of things" (verse 15)?
- Who are the "enemies of the cross of Christ" (verse 18)?
- Why are they enemies and what is their destiny, god, and glory? What do they mean?
- How are their minds on earthly things?

PHILIPPIANS 3:21-4:1

- Why is the Philippians' citizenship in heaven?
- What happens when we finally get there?
- How should the Philippians stand firm?
- Have you ever considered making the Christian life like a race or an athletic competition?
- What would your life look like if you did?

FINALLY...

- Anything in these verses that's a puzzle to you? That just doesn't make sense?
- What one thing got your attention most of all in these verses? Why did it affect you like it did?

Tour de Life

In the race of your life, what's your final goal? What are the markers along the way? What markers might show that you're on the wrong path? Where are you on the path? Use this diagram to picture your life as an endurance race.

THE
FINAL GOAL
Philippians 3:14
DO NOT ENTER
(What keeps you from God?)
(What behaviors do you need to give up?)
STOP
YIELD
(What mistakes do you want to avoid?)
(What is one good habit that you should begin in your life?)
THIS WAY
MERGE
(Who can help you grow in faith?)
(How did you become a Christian?)
ONE WAY

The Finish Line

Music and lyrics by Steve Taylor

Once upon an average morn
An average boy was born for the second time
Prone upon the altar there
He whispered up a prayer he'd kept hid inside
The vision came, he saw the odds
A hundred little gods on a gilded wheel
"These will vie to take your place
But, Father, by Your grace I will never kneel"

And I saw you, upright and proud
And I saw you wave to the crowd
And I saw you laughing out loud at the Philistines
And I saw you brush away rocks
And I saw you pull up your socks
And I saw you out on the blocks for the finish line

Darkness falls, the devil stirs
And as your vision blurs you start stumbling
The heart is weak, the will is gone
And every strong conviction comes tumbling down
Malice rains, the acid guile
Is sucking at your shoes while the mud is fresh
It floods the trail, it leaves you dry
As every little god buys its pound of flesh

And I saw you licking your wounds
And I saw you weave your cocoons
And I saw you changing your tunes for the party line
And I saw you welsh on old debts
I saw you and your comrades bum cigarettes
And you hemmed and you hawed
And you hedged all your bets waiting for a sign

Let's all wash our hands as we throw little fits
Let's all wash our hands as we curse hypocrites
We're locked in the washroom turning old tricks
Deaf and joyless and full of it

The vision came, he saw the odds
A hundred little gods on a gilded wheel
"These have tried to take Your place
But, Father, by Your grace, I will never kneel
I will never kneel"

Off in the distance, bloodied but wise
As you squint with the light of the truth in your eyes
And I saw you, both hands were raised
And I saw your lips move in praise
And I saw you steady your gaze for the finish line
Every idol like dust, a word scattered them all
And I rose to my feet when you scaled the last wall
And I gasped when I saw you fall in His arms at the finish line

resources from youth specialties

Youth Ministry Programming

Camps, Retreats, Missions, & Service Ideas (Ideas Library)
Creative Bible Lessons from the Old Testament
Creative Bible Lessons in 1 & 2 Corinthians
Creative Bible Lessons in Galatians and Philippians
Creative Bible Lessons in John: Encounters with Jesus
Creative Bible Lessons in Romans: Faith on Fire!
Creative Bible Lessons on the Life of Christ
Creative Bible Lessons in Psalms
Creative Junior High Programs from A to Z, Vol. 1 (A–M)
Creative Junior High Programs from A to Z, Vol. 2 (N–Z)
Creative Meetings, Bible Lessons, & Worship Ideas (Ideas Library)
Crowd Breakers & Mixers (Ideas Library) Downloading the Bible Leader's Guide
Drama, Skits, & Sketches (Ideas Library)
Drama, Skits, & Sketches 2 (Ideas Library)
Drama, Skits, & Sketches 3 (Ideas Library)
Dramatic Pauses
Everyday Object Lessons
Games (Ideas Library)
Games 2 (Ideas Library)
Games 3 (Ideas Library)
Good Sex: A Whole-Person Approach to Teenage Sexuality & God
Great Fundraising Ideas for Youth Groups
More Great Fundraising Ideas for Youth Groups
Great Retreats for Youth Groups
Great Talk Outlines for Youth Ministry
Holiday Ideas (Ideas Library)
Hot Illustrations for Youth Talks
More Hot Illustrations for Youth Talks
Still More Hot Illustrations for Youth Talks
Hot Illustrations for Youth Talks 4
Hot Illustrations CD-ROM
Ideas Library on CD-ROM
Incredible Questionnaires for Youth Ministry
Junior High Game Nights
More Junior High Game Nights
Kickstarters: 101 Ingenious Intros to Just about Any Bible Lesson
Live the Life! Student Evangelism Training Kit
Memory Makers
The Next Level Leader's Guide
Play It! Over 150 Great Games for Youth Groups
Roaring Lambs
Screen Play
So What Am I Gonna Do With My Life?
Special Events (Ideas Library)
Spontaneous Melodramas
Spontaneous Melodramas 2
Student Leadership Training Manual
Student Underground: An Event Curriculum on the Persecuted Church
Super Sketches for Youth Ministry
Talking the Walk
Teaching the Bible Creatively
Videos That Teach
What Would Jesus Do? Youth Leader's Kit
Wild Truth Bible Lessons
Wild Truth Bible Lessons 2
Wild Truth Bible Lessons—Pictures of God
Worship Services for Youth Groups

Professional Resources

Administration, Publicity, & Fundraising (Ideas Library)
Dynamic Communicators Workshop
Great Talk Outlines for Youth Ministry
Help! I'm a Junior High Youth Worker!
Help! I'm a Small-Group Leader!
Help! I'm a Sunday School Teacher!
Help! I'm an Urban Youth Worker!
Help! I'm a Volunteer Youth Worker!
How to Expand Your Youth Ministry
How to Speak to Youth...and Keep Them Awake at the Same Time
Junior High Ministry (Updated & Expanded)
The Ministry of Nurture: A Youth Worker's Guide to Discipling Teenagers
Postmodern Youth Ministry
Purpose-Driven® Youth Ministry
Purpose-Driven® Youth Ministry Training Kit
So *That's* Why I Keep Doing This! 52 Devotional Stories for Youth Workers
A Youth Ministry Crash Course
Youth Ministry Management Tools
The Youth Worker's Handbook to Family Ministry

Academic Resources

Four Views of Youth Ministry & the Church
Starting Right: Thinking Theologically About Youth Ministry
Youth Ministry That Transforms

Discussion Starters

Discussion & Lesson Starters (Ideas Library)
Discussion & Lesson Starters 2 (Ideas Library)
EdgeTV
Get 'Em Talking
Keep 'Em Talking!
Good Sex: A Whole-Person Approach to Teenage Sexuality & God
High School TalkSheets—Updated!
More High School TalkSheets—Updated!
High School TalkSheets from Psalms and Proverbs—Updated!
Junior High—Middle School TalkSheets—Updated!
More Junior High—Middle School TalkSheets—Updated!
Junior High—Middle School TalkSheets from Psalms and Proverbs—Updated!
Real Kids: Short Cuts
Real Kids: The Real Deal—on Friendship, Loneliness, Racism, & Suicide
Real Kids: The Real Deal—on Sexual Choices, Family Matters, & Loss
Real Kids: The Real Deal—on Stressing Out, Addictive Behavior, Great Comebacks, & Violence
Real Kids: Word on the Street
Unfinished Sentences: 450 Tantalizing Statement-Starters to Get Teenagers Talking & Thinking
What If...? 450 Thought-Provoking Questions to Get Teenagers Talking, Laughing, and Thinking
Would You Rather...? 465 Provocative Questions to Get Teenagers Talking
Have You Ever...? 450 Intriguing Questions Guaranteed to Get Teenagers Talking

Art Source Clip Art

Youth Group Activities (print)
Clip Art Library Version 2.0 (CD-ROM)

Digital Resources

Clip Art Library Version 2.0 (CD-ROM)
Great Talk Outlines for Youth Ministry
Hot Illustrations CD-ROM
Ideas Library on CD-ROM
Screen Play
Youth Ministry Management Tools

Videos & Video Curricula

Dynamic Communicators Workshop
EdgeTV
Live the Life! Student Evangelism Training Kit
Purpose-Driven® Youth Ministry Training Kit
Real Kids: Short Cuts
Real Kids: The Real Deal—on Friendship, Loneliness, Racism, & Suicide
Real Kids: The Real Deal—on Sexual Choices, Family Matters, & Loss
Real Kids: The Real Deal—on Stressing Out, Addictive Behavior, Great Comebacks, & Violence
Real Kids: Word on the Street
Student Underground: An Event Curriculum on the Persecuted Church
Understanding Your Teenager Video Curriculum
Youth Ministry Outside the Lines

Student Resources

Downloading the Bible: A Rough Guide to the New Testament
Downloading the Bible: A Rough Guide to the Old Testament
Grow For It Journal through the Scriptures
So What Am I Gonna Do With My Life?
Spiritual Challenge Journal: The Next Level
Teen Devotional Bible
What (Almost) Nobody Will Tell You about Sex
What Would Jesus Do? Spiritual Challenge Journal
Wild Truth Journal for Junior Highers
Wild Truth Journal—Pictures of God
Wild Truth Journal—Pictures of God 2